To most of us, life is complex. It is times, when things are mainstream they become wonderfully complex know one of those wonderful, autistic individuals that change our lives forever.

It might seem at times that everything is an up-hill battle, as Tayo describes in her book. Some people support and understand, others shun and judge. This is where we know who is with us no matter what.

In her book, Tayo takes us on a journey through her own life, as a single mother raising twin sons, one autistic, one neurotypical. The challenges were there, but so was the love. As we learn about Tayo, David and Jonathan, we also learn about autism, Nigerian culture, and the struggles of BAME communities.

That should be plenty, right?

Add meltdowns, communication difficulties, shame of being judged or rejected, misunderstanding behaviours that are communication rather than misbehaving, and we have a recipe for disaster. But Tayo and the twins took it in their stride.

Yes, it wasn't always easy but with supportive friends and family, they learned to ride the waves of meltdowns and judgement and make their lives the best they could.

Navigating the school system and getting David's needs met is an interesting dilemma I'm familiar with, having worked in care with people with Autism and learning disabilities for 11 years, and now as a counsellor with "high functioning" autistic adults, I know how hard it is to get a good social worker, and get what we need for our service users or our children.

I highly recommend this book. You'll be nodding away if you've got some - or a lot - of knowledge of autism, and you'll be very thankful you read it, if you're new to the world of Autism and Neurodiversity, because it will teach you a lot - Tayo has dedicated sections entitled "did you know" and "helpful hints" where you can put into practice the things your child might need at different points in their development, through Tayo's example in her own life story with her twins.

I was in tears in some bits, seeing how David's relationship with the world changed through time, how Jonathan learned from his brother - something I've experienced as well, I've learned a lot from the people I've supported. I've learned that life is simple, that it's easy, but us as humans complicate it. Yes, neurodiverse people might be complex, but if you take the time to really see them, you'll see they are wonderful and that you have a lot to learn from them. Jonathan's chapter, and the whole book really, teaches us that.

Everyone should read this. We need more understanding of our autistic people. We need to embrace them and learn from them. There's a lot to be learned. There's so much we don't know, but once we open our eyes, we will see these precious lives for what they are: wonderful and complex. Or like Tayo's book title says: Wonderfully Complex.

—Karin Brauner, Counsellor, Coach,
Clinical Supervisor. Author of 20 Self-Care Habits
and The Beckoning Rooms

Wonderfully Complex

Appreciating the Uniqueness of Your Autistic Child

TAYO IGBINTADE

WITH

JONATHAN OGUNDEJI

Wonderfully Complex © 2022 by Tayo Igbintade. All rights reserved.

Published by Author Academy Elite
PO Box 43, Powell, OH 43065
www.AuthorAcademyElite.com

All rights reserved. This book contains material protected under International and Federal Copyright Laws and Treaties. Any unauthorized reprint or use of this material is prohibited. No part of this book may be reproduced or transmitted in any form or by any means, electronic or mechanical, including photocopying, recording, or by any information storage and retrieval system, without express written permission from the author.

Identifiers:

LCCN: 2021925681

ISBN: 978-1-64746-983-2 (paperback)
ISBN: 978-1-64746-984-9 (hardback)
ISBN: 978-1-64746-985-6 (ebook)

Available in paperback, hardback, e-book, and audiobook

All Scripture quotations, unless otherwise indicated, are taken from the Holy Bible, New International Version®, NIV®. Copyright © 1973, 1978, 1984 by Biblica, Inc.™ Used by permission of Zondervan. All rights reserved worldwide.

Any Internet addresses (websites, blogs, etc.) and telephone numbers printed in this book are offered as a resource. They are not intended in any way to be or imply an endorsement by Author Academy Elite, nor does Author Academy Elite vouch for the content of these sites and numbers for the life of this book.

Some names and identifying details have been changed to protect the privacy of individuals.

Dedication

To my sons, David and Jonathan: I chose your names because I wanted you to have a strong, enduring relationship, just like your Biblical namesakes. I didn't realise how much you would live up to the meaning of your names.

David – Beloved of God; throughout your life, I've seen the demonstration of how much God loves you and is constantly with you.

Jonathan – Gift of God/God is gracious; God was gracious to our family when he gave you to me as my son. I'm proud of the man you've become and of your generous spirit.

I love you both, always and forever.

I praise you because I am fearfully and wonderfully made.

Psalms 139:14

Foreword

As parents, we want our children to be perfectly healthy and full of life. Lord knows we see them as our mini gorgeous perfect creature. As such, no parent wants to hear there may/could be something wrong with their child, much less something with no cure. We want our children to be special! We just don't want them to have special needs.

Raising children undoubtedly, is no easy feat, raising one with additional care and support is incredibly tough! It requires strength you never knew you had.

As a mother of a special needs child, I can relate with Tayo's story and the waves of emotions that often accompany having your child diagnosed with lifelong disability. The journey is a long and tedious one with many twists and turns. One quickly learns to appreciate and celebrate every milestone, no matter how small, it is never insignificant.

The reality for family with special need children is different and can be made more difficult having to deal with negative reactions and insensitivity from people who are oblivious to the challenges of their everyday life.

In this book, Tayo shares her story of triumph and struggles in raising her special child David and his twin brother Jonathan. Her vulnerability will open your eyes to the hidden wonder and beauty of raising a child with a disability in a world that is yet to fully understand them.

This is a must-read for everyone out there who wants to learn about supporting people who are raising a child with special needs and those parents raising their special child, you are not alone. It is beautifully written with insightful tips and helpful information to help you navigate the difficult roads and challenging turns ahead.

A massive well done to Tayo for this awesome piece. I highly recommend this book.

Revd Victoria Lawrence
CEO – Abigail Outreach Ministry

Every child is uniquely gifted and is placed on the earth for a purpose. They are not weird.

Contents

Dedication v
Foreword vii
Glossary of Terms xiii

Chapter 1 Ignorance Is Bliss 1
    The Calm before the Diagnosis
Did You Know? 7
    Twins in Yoruba Mythology
Helpful Hints 8
    Autism FAQS

Chapter 2 Snake Oil or Not? 10
    Looking for a Cure
Did You Know? 19
    Religion, Culture, Superstition, and Disability
Helpful Hints 21
    Accepting Your Child

Chapter 3 I Just Want a School.................. 22
    Navigating the Education System
    Did You Know?........................... 32
        Sending Children "Back Home"
    Helpful Hints........................... 34
        Building Your Tribe

Chapter 4 Why Isn't He Speaking?................ 36
    The Search for a Way to Communicate
    Did You Know?........................... 46
        Augmentative and Alternative Communication
    Helpful Hints........................... 47
        Effective Communication

Chapter 5 There's Nothing Wrong with Him; He's Just Naughty................................ 48
    Black and Autistic—Double Discrimination
    Did You Know?........................... 54
        Systemic Racism in the United Kingdom
    Helpful Hints........................... 56
        How to Make a Difference

Chapter 6 Oh No! He's Eloped................... 57
    Wanderlust
    Did You Know?........................... 65
        Elopement
    Helpful Hints........................... 66
        What To Do if Your Child Wanders

Chapter 7 Puberty and the Hormone Express........ 67
    Did You Know?........................... 83
        Tantrums and Meltdowns
    Helpful Hints........................... 85
        Keeping Your Child Safe

Chapter 8 School's Out Forever - What's Next?
Transition to adulthood. 87
    Did You Know?. 98
      Transitioning Is Difficult
    Helpful Hints. 100
      How to Ensure Successful Transition Planning

Chapter 9 The Empty Nest. 102
    Creating a New Normal after Your Children Move Out
    Did You Know?. 111
      Autism and Adults

Chapter 10 Why Is My Brother Like This?. 112
    A Sibling's Perspective, by Jonathan Ogundeji
    Helpful Hints. 138
      Supporting Your Autistic Child's Siblings

Chapter 11 When Your World Turns Upside Down. . . 140
    Dealing with the Unexpected & Planning for the Future
    Did You Know?. 147
      Legally Caring for Adults with Special Needs
    Helpful Hints. 149
      Making Plans for the Future

Afterword. 151
Bibliography. 155
Endnotes 159
Acknowledgements. 161
About the Author 163

Glossary of Terms

Autism—a lifelong developmental/neurological condition that affects how people communicate and interact with the world.

ASDAN—a curriculum development organisation and awarding body, providing courses that develop skills for learning, work, and life.

BAME—Black, Asian, and Minority Ethnic; all ethnic groups except White ethnic groups. It does not relate to the country of origin or affiliation.

British Sign Language (BSL)—the language of the Deaf community in the UK, involving a combination of hand shapes, facial expressions, lip pattern, and body language.

CAMHS—Child and Adolescent Mental Health Services: A service that provides support to children and adolescents who are struggling with their mental health.

Child Protection Register—a confidential register held by each local authority consisting of every child or young person in their area considered to be suffering from or likely to suffer significant harm.

Deputyship—where a person has lost the ability to look after their affairs but has not set up a Power of Attorney beforehand, their carers can apply to the Court of Protection, and a deputy will be appointed to look after the person's affairs. There are two types of deputies: one for property and financial issues, and one for personal welfare.

Developmental delay—delay in reaching language, thinking, social, or motor skill milestones.

DSM-5—the Diagnostic and Statistical Manual of Mental Health Disorders is a standard classification of mental disorders used by mental health professionals.

Early Years Centre—a child development centre that offers assessments, diagnostic services, family support and information services, outreach and play and leisure services aimed at children that have been referred by the National Health.

Echolalia—the repetition of words and phrases that have been heard by the autistic individual.

Education, Health and Care Plan (ECH/ECHP)—a legal document that describes a child or young person's Special Educational Needs (SEN) and/or Disabilities (SEND). The ECHP replaced the Statement of Special Educational Needs in 2014.

Elopement—the tendency to wander or run aware from secure settings. This is common in autistic children and adults with dementia.

Exclusion (from education)—there are two types of exclusion in the UK. Fixed period exclusion, where a child is suspended from school for a specified number of days, up to a maximum of forty-five days, and permanent exclusion, where a child is expelled from school and not allowed to return.

Guardianship—obtaining legal authority from the courts to make decisions on behalf of another person who is unable to make decisions in their best interests, provide for their own welfare, and unwilling or unable to sign a durable power of attorney. The guardian has the power to manage property, finances, and personal welfare.

Glue ear—a condition where the middle ear becomes filled with a sticky fluid that causes temporary hearing loss. It is a common ailment in young children.

Idioglossia—an autonomous/private language created and spoken by an individual/group of individuals. Idioglossia commonly occurs with twins (also known as twin talk, twin speech, or cryptophasia), but they usually outgrow it.

Individual Education Plan (IEP)—a document that contains planning, teaching, and reviewing tools used by schools to help children with special educational needs access and engage with the curriculum.

Local authority (also referred to as the Council)—a structure of local government in the UK that is responsible for social care, schools, housing, and planning amongst other services.

Makaton—a language programme that combines the use of signs, symbols, and speech to enable people with learning difficulties to communicate.

Means tested—when a person's income is assessed to determine whether they are eligible to receive benefits or services.

MMR—the combined measles, mumps, and rubella vaccine. A report by Andrew Wakefield [1] and others (which has since been discredited) reported links between receiving the vaccine and the onset of autism.

Nonverbal—the inability to speak or develop spoken language other than a few words or phrases.

Power of attorney—a legal document where a person nominates a trusted friend or relative to look after their affairs if they lose the capacity to do it themselves. The person must have the capacity to make this decision for it to be granted.

Residential School—a boarding school where children live and study and return home at the end of the week/ term.

Respite Care— A care provider which specialises in providing short-term care for individuals with special needs so that their primary carers can take a break from their caring responsibilities.

Statement of Special Needs (also referred to as Statement)—a legally binding document setting out a child/young person's special educational needs, the provision they require, and the educational placement they should attend.

Special Educational Needs—learning difficulties or disabilities that make it more difficult for children to learn than their peers.

Special Education Needs and Disabilities (SEND)—a child/young person aged between 0–25 years who has a learning difficulty or disability which means it's harder for them to learn than the peers and who require special educational provision.

Special Educational Needs Coordinator (SENCO)—someone who arranges the extra support needed by children/young people with special educational needs or disability; they are based in all mainstream schools and maintained nursery schools.

Social Care/Social Services—Social Care, previously known as Social Services, is a department in the local authority who have a statutory duty to safeguard the welfare of vulnerable children and adults and provide a wide range of services to children and families.

Speech and Language Therapy (SALT)—treatment, care, and support for children and adults who have difficulties with communication, eating, drinking, or swallowing.

Sensory Processing Disorder—a condition affecting how the brain processes sensory information (such as smell, taste, sight, sand, touch). It can affect one or more of the senses and can manifest in oversensitivity or undersensitivity to stimuli. (Examples: clothes feel too itchy, lights are too bright, food textures are uncomfortable, sounds are too loud, etc.)

Self-injurious behaviour—behaviour resulting in physical injury to one's own body, such as head banging, hand biting, skin picking, etc. It can occur due to being upset/frustrated, to gain attention, or can be a way of self-stimulating.

Stimming—self-stimulating, repetitive behaviour/sounds such as rocking, flapping, or spinning. It is often engaged in as a self-soothing activity but can sometimes be harmful and veer into self-injurious behaviour.

Tribunal – the First Tier Tribunal or SEND Tribunal is an independent national tribunal in the United Kingdom where young people and their parents can appeal decisions that have been made by their Local Authority concerning their special educational needs.

Vaccine damage—an adverse event caused by a vaccine. It could be producing the infection that the vaccine is supposed to prevent; damage from toxic material (such as mercury) found in the vaccine or cause an allergy or autoimmune response.

CHAPTER 1

Ignorance Is Bliss

The Calm before the Diagnosis

I was pregnant! Deep in the recesses of my mind, I'd known for a while. As a Christian, this wasn't the way things were supposed to go. Abortion wasn't an option, and I didn't have any friends I could talk to or ask for advice. At twenty-three, naïve, and having lived a fairly sheltered life, I didn't know what to do. So, I carried on with life in a full-fledged state of denial, going to work each day and hoping that pretending I wasn't pregnant would make it true.

After a ten-year stint in Nigeria, I returned to the United Kingdom and was staying with relatives in London. When I started to show, I wore baggy clothes to disguise my growing bump. One day, a visitor asked me when I was due; the cat was truly out of the bag! Nigerian families have rigid views on how life should be lived: Education is the number one priority (preferably a university degree), then marriage to someone from a good family (a big society wedding), *then* babies. My situation did not follow the plan!

I had to call home to tell the rest of my family before word got back to them. It was important they heard it from me: I was pregnant, had secretly gotten married, and had already been deserted. Needless to say, they were shocked. I had been the poster girl for my family—the goody-two-shoes who rarely went out because I was always home studying. I had been the one held up for my siblings and cousins as a role model. My family had such high hopes and huge expectations of me. Nobody could understand how I ended up in that situation. Once the initial shock wore off, my friends and family rallied around me and supported me. For that, I was thankful. I had realised early on that the father was not going to be involved in the life of my unborn child; without God and my family, I would have been completely on my own.

My easy, uneventful pregnancy gave me no indication of just how much my life was about to change. I went for an antenatal check-up soon after I acknowledged I was pregnant. The doctor thought I was further along than I believed and sent me to get an ultrasound scan. To my shock and dismay, I saw two babies on the scan!

As my belly grew, I wondered how I would cope. I had never been the maternal type, and now I had two babies growing inside me. My unhappiness bordered on despair. Still in denial, I carried on working until two weeks before I was due. I was healthy, slim, and fit. Apart from heartburn, severe anaemia (which was dealt with by tripling my iron tablet intake), and waddling like a duck, I experienced no issues. Towards the end of my pregnancy, people would comment about my huge belly, asking how many babies I was carrying.

My due date was December twenty-fifth, so I'd been trying to come up with twin names (for their first names) that were Christmassy but not too cheesy. I'd tentatively looked at Emmanuel and Noel, Emmanuel and Stella, and Stella and

Carol (the hospital had refused to tell me the sex of the babies). I wasn't entirely happy with those names, but that's what I was working with. As twins, they would automatically be named Taiwo and Kehinde as per Yoruba (a Nigerian tribe) culture.

The week before my due date, I went to St Thomas's Hospital for my usual antenatal check-up. The doctor took one look at me and, and insisted I stay in the hospital overnight. He scheduled me for an induction the next day. Doctors generally don't advise allowing pregnancies of twins or multiples to go full term as complications frequently arise. On the morning of 19 December 1990, the doctor induced labour and at 7:10 p.m., my first son was born naturally; unfortunately, his twin brother turned around and was lying sideways, with his hand coming down towards the birth canal, so I had to have an emergency C-section. My friend, Adeola, had arrived to support me during the labour and was cooing over her new godson while they wheeled me into surgery theatre. When I came around from the C-section, I saw my younger brother, Axe, who told me, "The second one is a boy." Still a bit groggy from the anaesthetic I replied, "What second one?"

I stayed in hospital over Christmas and finally decided on names for my identical twin sons: David and Jonathan. I wanted them to be best friends like their biblical namesakes. I fell in love with them instantly and knew from the moment I laid my eyes on them, I would do anything for them. I finally understood everything I'd ever read and heard about a mother's love. I was amazed at how I'd managed to produce these two little people (and carry the weight of two six-pound babies inside me).

When I left the hospital on 27 December, reality finally hit—*how on earth was I going to look after two babies on my own?* I had stitches from a tear, as well as the C-section, and had been instructed not to carry anything heavy, but I had two babies. It wasn't easy. Luckily, I had the support of my brother Axe, who lived with me at the time; he was the closest thing my boys had to a father.

Like most new-borns, my sons didn't sleep through the night. While most new parents could find reprieve during feeding time, mine wouldn't feed at the same time, so I had to alternate bottle feeding one and while I breastfed the other—exhausting. One day, both babies were crying, and nothing I would do would get them to stop. In frustration, I left them in the room, went to another room, and broke down crying. Concerned, my brother came in to check on me. He left quietly and took care of the twins. I felt so disheartened and didn't know how I would be able to raise them.

My mother was a godsend. She came from Nigeria when the twins were two weeks old and stayed for the first year of their lives. She got them both sleeping through the night (from 11 p.m. until about 5:30 or 6-ish), and for that, I am eternally grateful. Looking back on my state of mind during the boys' first month, I can fully understand how sleep deprivation is used as an effective method of torturing people.

I went back to work at Royal Mail when the boys were four months old, and things seemed to be progressing well. The boys passed all their milestones; they walked at ten months of age and started snoring. At last, I was able to relax. I watched my beautiful babies sleep; sometimes they were so still, I wondered if they were still alive! I'd shake them awake, just to make sure. I was starting to get into the rhythm of motherhood. David was outgoing, sociable, and boisterous. His charm made it easy for him to get people to do anything for him by smiling at them—his smile was really something to behold. Jonathan, on the other hand, was quieter and a bit clingy, but he adored his brother and would follow him everywhere as they grew older. My friends loved them almost as much as I did.

I wasn't too concerned about their lack of speech when they were supposed to start talking. I had read all the baby magazines zealously and noted that twins typically tend to be late speakers and sometimes develop Idioglossia—their own unique twin language. They started to say their first baby words shortly before their second birthday; then Jonathan's speech started to develop, but David seemed to regress. He wouldn't always respond to his name, and things didn't seem quite right.

Still, I wasn't too worried at this stage; I assumed he had glue ear and took him to see the doctor. My GP sent him for hearing tests at the Early Years Centre in Siward Road, Tooting; after the test, the doctor told me his hearing was excellent, but he appeared to have developmental delay. This was when worry washed over me, and I asked so many questions but I wouldn't know the answers until further tests were done.

I started reading voraciously any literature I could find on developmental delay in toddlers. At this point, the twins were just over two and a half years old. One day while reading either *Woman's Own* or *Woman Magazine*, I came across an article about a mother who had sent her autistic daughter to the Higashi School (for autism) in Boston—alarm bells started going off in my head. Many of the behaviours described in the article mirrored what I saw in David. At the time, I hadn't heard of autism or seen an autistic person before. When I asked people whether they thought David was autistic, the general response was "artistic?" I would have to explain my limited understanding of autism.

The walking on tiptoes, which I thought was cute, was one of the possible indications of autism. The finger flicking, rocking, endless spinning, taking my hand and throwing it in the direction of the item he wanted instead of pointing—all these were signs of autism. Jonathan also displayed some of the same behaviours, but I later realised he was copying his brother. I made an appointment at the Early Years Centre and asked if David had autism. They seemed hesitant to confirm my suspicions until I assured them that I wouldn't freak out; I just wanted to know what I was dealing with.

The doctors' office referred me to Child Psychiatry at St. George's Hospital where David was under the care of Dr Jeremy Turk. I can't remember what went on during those appointments. To be honest, my memories of that time are fuzzy. I remember them giving him items to play with and asking me how he typically played at home and how he interacted with his brother. They also ran some tests to see if he could recognise and name various objects. I clearly remember when they showed David a picture of a violin, his response was "gita"—I didn't realise he knew what a guitar was! After many sessions, they finally diagnosed David with classic autism, and told me if he wasn't talking by the age of six, he would never talk. They also said he would probably need institutional care his whole life.

My whole world collapsed. My first thought was God would not allow this to happen to me. I was devastated and couldn't believe there was something wrong with my child. My beautiful boy had a disability. I just couldn't comprehend what they had told me. It didn't help that autism wasn't a well-known disorder—there weren't any guidebooks on what to expect or what to do. The subsequent years felt like I was fumbling around in the dark. My period of blissful ignorance was over. A whole new chapter of my life was about to start.

Did You Know?

Twins in Yoruba Mythology

There seems to be a universal fascination surrounding twins, especially identical twins. Some parts of the world are renown for having clusters of twins or an unusually high concentration of twin births compared to the norm—for instance Candida Godoi in Brazil and Kodihini in India. But West Africa has the highest prevalence of twins globally, particularly the Yoruba tribe, located in Benin, Nigeria, and Togo.

The birth of twins is considered a special event, and before the spread of Christianity and Islam in Africa, people made sacrifices to the twin deity. Twins were revered as being divine and thought to be capable of bringing prosperity or misery to their family and people around them. The fear surrounding twins was so great that up until the early 19th century, many twins were killed at birth or left in the forest to die. Mary Slessor, a Scottish missionary to Nigeria, is credited with ending the practice of twin infanticide in Nigeria. However, very occasionally, stories are still told about people who have ritually sacrificed and killed twins in the hope of becoming rich and prosperous.

These days, twins are celebrated, and people often treat them favourably, giving them gifts to benefit from the prosperity and good fortune they bring. However, many people still believe if you mistreat twins, you bring a curse upon yourself.

Helpful Hints
Autism FAQS

What is autism?

The National Autistic Society (NAS)[2] defines autism as "a lifelong, developmental disability that affects how a person communicates and relates to other people, and how they relate to the world around them." It generally tends to be noticed around the age of three.

Are there levels of autism?

Low functioning vs. high functioning? Autism is regarded as a spectrum, and the diagnoses frequency given is Autistic Spectrum Disorder (ASD). In the past, people were diagnosed with Asperger syndrome, PDD-NOS (Pervasive Developmental Disorder-Not Otherwise Specified), and Autism, but these have been replaced with ASD in the Diagnostic and Statistical Manual of Mental Health Disorders, 5th Edition[3] (DSM-5). People anecdotally talk about low functioning and high functioning, but this is not clinically defined.

What causes autism?

The simple answer is nobody knows what causes autism. There are various theories, but nothing proved or evidenced. However, it is generally accepted that there is a genetic element to the prevalence of autism.

What are the symptoms of autism? When diagnosing autism, the experts[4] usually refer to a triad of impairments that "limit and impair everyday functioning." These impairments affect:

1. Social interactions—these manifest in difficulty understanding social norms and the unwritten rules governing social interactions and behaviours.

2. Social communication—this is evidenced by difficulty in verbal and nonverbal communication, not being able to understand the meaning of everyday gestures, facial expressions, etc.

3. Rigidity of thinking and difficulties with social imagination—this plays out in problems with interpersonal play and imagination: having a limited number of imaginative activities, which are repeated rigidly.

All autistic people have difficulties in these three areas to differing degrees.

Can autism be cured?

No, it's a lifelong neurological condition. However, early intervention can help an autistic child better navigate the world.

How common is autism? Autism is found in just over 2% of the population[5]. Boys are four times more likely to be autistic than girls. It occurs across all ethnic and socioeconomic groups.

CHAPTER 2

Snake Oil or Not?

Looking for a Cure

I don't clearly remember the days after the diagnosis—they went by in a blur. How could I explain something I didn't quite understand myself? My friends and family were supportive in their own way but couldn't help me. I was grieving for something I had always taken for granted—having a "normal" child. The responses I would get when I tried to explain his condition included: "But he's not deaf." "There's nothing wrong with him; you're being an overprotective mum." "Did you say he's artistic?" "It's your fault, you must have sinned." "Maybe it was something you did when you were pregnant," and many more.

Autism is sometimes called the invisible disability; when you look at an autistic child, there isn't anything apparently different. But when they start talking or displaying certain behaviours, they may appear a little odd or even naughty. It's difficult to explain their behaviour when you don't understand it yourself. You just know that they can't help it, they're not being wilfully difficult or naughty, but they are just doing the best they can in a world that doesn't make a lot of sense to them.

When he was about three and a half, David was diagnosed with "classic autism with challenging behaviour." I had the mixed blessing of having Jonathan, his doppelganger, to compare him to. I would see Jonathan achieving various milestones while his brother lagged behind him. Watching Jonathan develop and flourish while David seemed to regress was heart-breaking. I found it incredibly difficult to see what appeared to be a split personality play out before me in two children.

David was so hyperactive! He was a bundle of energy—he seemed to move in a blur; it was so difficult to keep up with him. Despite his autism, he was the leader, and his brother was the follower. He was a typical adventurous child. I remember seeing him wake up and watching him through half-closed eyes as he performed his morning ritual. He would shake his brother awake, climb out of his cot bed, and then motion for his brother to follow. Jonathan would often fall trying to climb out of the cot. They would make their way to the bedroom door before I intercepted them and stopped them in their tracks.

Looking back, I remember how David often tried to get the better of the stair gate. One time, he managed to climb over it and fell down the stairs. I nearly had a heart attack. Little did I know that this was a foreshadow of the many escapades and adventures he would have as a boy growing up.

I kept myself busy, trying to find out what could have caused it. I read voraciously anything I could find about autism. I discovered autism was also known as Kanner's syndrome, after the American Psychiatrist who did a lot of the early research into autism. Leo Kanner[4] attributed the cause of autism in children to their emotionless refrigerator mothers who didn't show maternal warmth towards their children. I already felt a lot of guilt, as I suffered from low self-esteem, and felt inadequate for not being able to carry a "normal" child. I knew in my head that this was illogical – after all, Jonathan was fine! It felt like a punishment for falling away from my faith as a Christian for a short time—it was during this period I met the twin's father and became pregnant.

Another theory I came across was vaccine damage, which I believed could explain

why David was autistic and Jonathan wasn't. From an early age, I noticed David's immune system wasn't as strong as his brother's. He'd catch every childhood illness going, but Jonathan would be fine, even though they shared the same bed, clothes, and space. David had a chest infection at three months old and was hospitalised for two weeks. When I heard about Dr Andrew Wakefield and his theory about the MMR vaccination being responsible for the apparent growth in the incidence of autism in the western world, it resonated with me. Even though he's been professionally discredited, and his theory has been debunked, my personal view is there's something to it. Perhaps the big pharmaceutical companies have suppressed the information because of the large amounts of money at stake. Looking back, I would still give my children all their jabs but would delay them if I felt they were unwell at the time. I might also consider giving them the injections singly, as opposed to the combined one. I want to clarify that I have no evidence that this is the case; I just strongly believe that it's a possibility.

There's a genetic element according to everything I've learned, as autism can and does run in families. In my experience, it seems there is a genetic predisposition, and under the right combination of circumstances, autism can occur. The twins were involved in a research project conducted by the Medical Research Council (MRC) in the UK on 100 sets of twins (identical and fraternal), where one or both were autistic. They were trying to identify whether there were differences between the autistic and non-autistic twins at a chromosomal level. However, their findings were inconclusive.

I learned that a traumatic birth experience could sometimes cause autism; however, if that was the case, Jonathan should have been the autistic child, as he was the one born by an emergency C-section.

I realised I would probably never find out why David was autistic, so I focused my efforts on finding a cure. As a good Christian, my first thought was prayer. So, I prayed and prayed and prayed. And prayed some more. And carried on praying. I knew God would answer me; I had so much confidence and faith. At first. Then, I started getting discouraged and wondered what I was doing wrong.

My church and Christian friends provided me with a wealth of support, but they were also a source of much of my discouragement and despair. Quick tip—if you don't know what to say to someone who has a "special need" or disabled child, say one of these two statements (or don't say anything):

"I'm praying for you." or "What do you need from me?"

Those were the statements I found most helpful. Other statements were very damaging, such as telling me my son was born this way because: there was sin in my life; he has an evil spirit that needs to be cast out; I had an unforgiving spirit; I must have done something terrible; I came from a bad family; or I was a terrible mother. If it weren't for a few truly Christian friends, I would've completely lost my faith and left Christianity altogether. I found the so-called "sinners" more supportive than many Christians, who made me feel condemned and judged.

In hindsight and reflecting on my interactions with other parents of children with special needs, I'm unsure how I remained a regular churchgoer. Many of my fellow parents of special needs children stopped attending their churches, temples, or mosques. The struggle was too hard; and the lack of empathy, the disapproving looks, muttered statements, and the rejection proved too much to handle. I used to wonder why my friends would put other parents in contact with me for advice and support (and still do)—I didn't have it all together. People would ask about how to get support to help their children get into specialist schools; resources or grants for special equipment or support; how to get respite services, a break, practical support, and sometimes they just wanted to talk to someone who understood what they were going through, and wouldn't judge them or their children.

I was so focused on trying to do the best for my son that I eventually grew a thick skin and sometimes was truly oblivious to people's attitudes and behaviours until they were pointed out to me by my outraged friends. People made snide remarks about the sins I must have committed that resulted in having an autistic child, excluded me from social gatherings and celebrations, and generally made me feel uncomfortable in their presence. Over the years, most churches I belonged to were supportive and welcoming of David and his quirks. However, at one church, I was asked to tie David to his seat and gag him as he was disturbing the rest of the congregation. At the time, only 10–12 people were in attendance, and they all knew David well. It was a newly established church, and the building had an echo that David loved to hear. I ignored those requests and stopped attending when they asked for David to take a "holiday" from church.

Unfortunately, in 2021, not much has changed. There's an occasional church with fantastic support for families with a child with disabilities, but this tends to be an anomaly and not the norm. Andrew Whitehead[5] conducted some research into church attendance among people with disabilities. His results were published in June 2018 and show that "children with chronic health conditions that impede communication and social interaction are most likely never to attend religious worship services." He cites Carter[6] in his research, who lists barriers to inclusion in church services for people with chronic health problems or chronically disabled children, including: architecture (building design and layout), attitudes, communication, programme design, and liturgy (the rituals and language used in church services).

I find it ironic—as a Christian, the church should have been a sanctuary for me, somewhere I could find solace and comfort. In reality, I often felt even more isolated and alone. It usually felt there was no place for me, and no-one cared about my sons and me.

In decades past, many cures were being touted, but since the growth of the internet age, it has grown worse. Currently, I don't look out to see the latest intervention or programme. But I have tried three different approaches to try and cure my son.

Special Diets:

Popular science hailed the gluten-free/casein-free as the greatest thing that would help autistic children become normal again. I bought the books, went to a couple of workshops, and gave it a try—and failed miserably! David, like many other autistic children, was an extremely fussy eater. So picky, in fact, that up till the age of about twelve, he would only eat rice, pasta, bread, and chips. I took him to see the doctor; I was so worried about his nutrition, but the doctor told me not to be concerned because he was still drinking lots of milk and getting most of what his body needed most. David would not touch any of the gluten-free/casein-free food I prepared for him. He would sniff at the food and push the plate away. I persisted for about a month, but he wouldn't budge. So, that was a bust and a huge waste of money. I now realise his eating habits were probably due to his sensory processing issues, and in hindsight, would have approached things very differently. I know some children have benefited from this approach, and I wouldn't dismiss it out of hand; however, it wasn't for David.

Special Drugs:

One of the things I came across in my search for a cure was a so-called miracle drug called secretin which was said to show massive improvements in behaviour within a few weeks. I went online, and I'm ashamed to say against my better judgement and at considerable expense, bought some vials of secretin. Unfortunately, it made no difference at all; once again, I was out of pocket with nothing to show. Looking back, this was incredibly reckless behaviour; anything could've been in those vials. It never ceases to amaze me the lengths to which unscrupulous people will go to fleece desperate parents trying to help their children. I thank God that none of my misguided behaviour harmed my son.

Special Programmes:

When the boys were about eight or nine years old, the BBC showed a documentary/film called *Son-Rise: A Miracle of Love* about a boy cured of his autism through a programme developed by his parents, Barry and Samaria Kaufman. After watching it, I researched and discovered the Options Institute in America ran a programme called the Son-Rise Program based on the principles shown in the film. The concept sounded like the perfect place for David, but I was a single mother who worked for the mail sorting centre in London. The costs to travel, stay, and attend the program were considerable. With the help of my fellow "posties," we put together several fundraisers to help raise the funds. We ran a 10K mini marathon to raise money through sponsorship; I say we ran, but I walked most of it and came in third to last (I'm very proud of the fact that I completed the run). Another friend, Gus, put on a work-out-athon to raise money; and a levy was organised and collected from my colleagues who were of Nigerian descent. They raised all the funds I needed for our flights, stay, and programme fee. A big shout out to the Royal Mail Nine Elms Crew for everything they did for me! I'm truly grateful for their support.

We arrived in Massachusetts and went through the week-long intensive programme. I learned a lot from it and tried to implement it on my return home; ultimately, I couldn't sustain it as it required a heavy investment of time and finances that I just couldn't give. It borrowed heavily from Applied Behaviour Analysis (ABA). Some of the things I learned and took away with me were:

- ❖ To accept my child for who he is.
- ❖ To try and join him in his world to engage with him on his terms.
- ❖ Not to see his stimming (self-stimulations—rocking, spinning, flapping) as a nuisance, but as a tool to help him cope in a world that he finds confusing and overwhelming.

During this time, well-meaning family and friends told me about itinerant men of God, evangelists, and Pastors with healing ministries and urged me to take David for healing prayers. I was reluctant to do this; I believed my prayers, as well as those of my pastor and church members, should have been enough to get God's attention. And I wasn't keen on the ministries of those men, especially the ones who had public deliverance services. On one occasion, my friends from work told me about a pastor with a healing ministry who I should go and see. I was reluctant, but they insisted and practically forced me to go and see him. Against my better judgement, I agreed, and my fears were realised. The ministry team was praying for people who were screaming and writhing on the ground, vomiting up various substances, while the service was going on. After the service and before the minister would pray for us, we had to buy his book at the price of £10. When I finally got to see him, I said I needed prayers for my son. He told me there was nothing wrong with the boy, and I was the problem. I would have to come back for eight days of prayer and six days of deliverance. Needless to say, I left and never went back.

After searching for various "solutions" over the years, I came to accept David as the uniquely created person he is. Yes, I would love to be able to sit down and have deep, riveting conversations with him. I'm sad to think he won't get married and have children of his own, but I have learned to appreciate his humour, passion for justice and fairness, and his outgoing, sociable, gregarious nature. My job is to do my best to prepare him to be comfortable in a world not designed for neurodiversity. I no longer search out the latest "cures" or treatments. Yes, my son is different from most people, but he is a loving, caring, funny human being who has blessed and enriched my life.

Today, David attends church regularly and is a well-liked member of our congregation. He enjoys the service, and I believe more people know his name than they do mine. He knows everything that is going on in the life of the church and regularly reminds me of events that he wants to be involved in. He feels accepted and at home, and that's the way it should be.

Did You Know?

Religion, Culture, Superstition, and Disability

Sometimes, it's difficult to understand why people behave the way they do when interacting with autistic children. However, our upbringing and society colours how we see the world and how we react and deal with people every day. Intersectionality is a buzzword commonly used these days, especially when dealing with issues of diversity and inclusion. We now understand that every part of a person's identity is important.

For black people, especially those with African heritage, religion, culture, and superstition have a huge and sometimes subtle influence on how we see and treat people with disabilities.

Some definitions:

Culture—a set of shared attitudes, beliefs, values, goals, and practices that characterises an institution, organisation, or a group

Religion—can be part of culture and may be defined as a belief in the existence of a deity or a supernatural power, a being who created and controls the universe, and is worshiped as a basis of that faith.

Superstition—a belief or way of behaving based on fear of the unknown or the belief that certain events or things will bring good or bad luck

These three concepts are intertwined, and it's often difficult to separate one from another. People who are devout Christians or Muslims still mix elements of their culture into their religious practice and may still believe irrational, superstitious things ingrained from a young age. These beliefs and mind-sets often influence attitudes and behaviours at the subconscious level.

When exploring the causes of disabilities—whether physical, sensory, or neurological—under the lens of culture, religion, and superstition, there are some recurring themes. People believe these conditions could be a curse from God, a result of family sins, due to ancestral violations, a punishment from the local deities, because of wicked deeds in a previous life (karma), a consequence of witchcraft, or demonstrating possession by evil spirits.

Unsurprisingly, these kinds of beliefs result in a range of attitudes displayed to those who are disabled. Attitudes such as fear, ignorance, pity, anxiety, superiority, horror, disgust, overprotection, patronisation, and sympathy come to mind. Beliefs and attitudes lead to behaviours that are out of place in a civilised society.

There are many extreme examples of negative behaviour shown to disabled people, particularly in Africa and the developing nations; not everyone treats disabled people this way, but this behaviour is generally overlooked or considered the norm. On the lower end of the scale, children are neglected, denied access to education, healthcare, and eventually employment. Their families segregate them during social interactions—it's not unheard of for friends and colleagues to be completely unaware of the existence of the disabled child. But these unfortunate individuals are also likely to be the object of violence, exploitation, rape, involuntary sterilisation, murder, and ritual killings. The superstitious beliefs that disabled people are connected to witchcraft, demonic influences, or are sub-human appear to justify this maltreatment; the stories of ritual abuse and horrific exorcism practices we hear from time to time on the news can all be linked back to superstitious, irrational beliefs.

Some countries are trying to educate their citizens about the rights of disabled people and the responsibility of the wider community to treat them in an equitable way, but it may take generations for these ingrained attitudes to shift.

Helpful Hints

Accepting Your Child

When I came to terms with the fact David was autistic and this was an intrinsic part of him, I started to enjoy my child.

David is very sociable and outgoing, unlike me. He's also full of life and energy. For my own sanity and David's well-being, we would go to the park where he and Jonathan would run and play. They would ride their bikes, and after a couple of hours, they would be tired out, and we'd return home for a peaceful evening. I was happy that I didn't have this hyperactive child running rings around me, and David got to spend quality time with his brother, having fun and expressing himself physically.

Today, David still enjoys swimming every week, going for long walks in the park, and doing gardening work. In 2015, David joined me and some of my work colleagues in climbing Mount Snowdon—the highest mountain in Wales—to raise money for charity. He raised double the amount I raised, and the whole family was proud of his achievements. David also enjoys puzzles and word searches; when we have to wait for appointments or are going on long trips, he always has one to hand to help him stay calm and focussed.

Working to your child's strengths and the things he loves will help build his self-esteem and confidence. David, like myself, is a perfectionist and a people pleaser. He wants to be independent and do things by himself but becomes incredibly frustrated when things don't turn out the way he would like. Reassuring him that the next time will be better and showing him that Jonathan and I don't always get things right seems to help.

Ultimately, every child is uniquely designed, and all they want is to be accepted and loved for who they are. I believe this is the easiest and hardest part of being a parent, but we can love and accept our children while still wanting the best for them.

CHAPTER 3

I Just Want a School

Navigating the Education System

The twins went to a playgroup not too long before attending the Early Years Centre, where David received his diagnosis. The contrast between David and the other children's behaviour first gave me an inkling that something was wrong. I had returned to work as a postwoman four months after their birth and was working the late shift—2 p.m.–10 p.m. My siblings and I all lived together at the time, and we had a system; whoever arrived home first would collect the twins. I would make sure I'd left everything they needed—their food, nightclothes, etc. were ready for them. I even got my brother's friend and his siblings who lived nearby involved. Without this support network, I wouldn't have been able to carry on working. The manager of the playgroup made a referral to the Early Years Centre for both boys, as Jonathan was also behind in his speech, so they started to go to both the playgroup and the Early Years Centre for support and assessments. They settled into a routine that continued for a few months.

Everything changed the year of their fifth birthday. In the United Kingdom, every child has to be in school or registered education provision by the school year when they turn five. Everything was going reasonably well for – at least for Jonathan; I had found a primary school near to the playgroup for him, so he started in the infants (similar to preschool). This was just before they were expected to start compulsory education, as they were 4 years old at of the beginning of September. It marked the beginning of years of struggles with the local authority education department in finding a school for David.

It's difficult enough finding a suitable school for your child under normal circumstances but throw a child with Special Education Needs into the mix, and it's nearly impossible. David was non-verbal, and he was still in nappies; this meant mainstream education with a classroom assistant was out of the question. The local authority was willing to place him in a special school for children with a wide range of needs—physical, sensory, and learning disabilities. We attended the school for an assessment, and I didn't feel that it would be a good fit for David. The headmistress felt the same. The class they intended to put David in had several physically frail children, and the headmistress told me in over twenty years of teaching, she had never seen a child as hyperactive as David. She felt he would be a danger to some of the other more vulnerable children, and so ended our exploration of that school.

By this time, I had become a member of Contact-A-Family, a charity that supports families who have any kind of disability. They provide information, advice, and support and facilitate local support groups. My local chapter helped me identify a good school in a neighbouring local authority, but the education department in my area wasn't willing to pay for David to go there. They proposed sending him to a year-long residential school in Hampshire (which didn't make any sense to me as that would be far more expensive). I'm assuming they saw the look on my face and told me to go away and think about it.

I did some research and realised the school they had put forward catered for the most complex cases of autism and children with severe "challenging behaviour." It amazed me they thought it was appropriate for a four-year-old child to move to a boarding school located sixty-five miles away without the option to come home often. Needless to say, I did not take them up on this offer. Over the years, I've often thought about this time and reflected on why I was so adamant that I didn't want David to go to a residential school. I believe my own experiences of boarding school may have influenced my feelings. I did not enjoy my time at a secondary boarding school in Nigeria. I was very shy and was treated badly by my fellow students and the staff. As a result, I wasn't willing to send my vulnerable son to a residential school, especially as I felt he had no way of telling me if people were not treating him well. I also believed that David would thrive in the midst of positive role models and didn't believe that placing him with the worst of the worst (as I saw it at the time) would help him in the slightest.

Some friends and acquaintances advised me to send David "back home" to Nigeria so that I could focus my efforts on Jonathan. A few suggested I send Jonathan instead, as there would be more provision for an autistic child in the UK. It was common for British-born Nigerians to send their children back to Nigeria to stay with their extended family. Sometimes, children truanting, causing trouble in school, rebelling, acting disobediently, being promiscuous, or who are at risk of joining a gang are sent to be in a more structured, authoritarian environment back home. Also, childcare costs are high, so sending a child to Nigeria and providing financial support for them is seen as a sensible financial option for some parents.

My friends were thinking of my well-being, my ability to work and support my children, and my ability to have a relationship with someone in the future, unhindered by my baggage of a child with special needs. However, as a mother, I felt it was my responsibility to take care of my child; I didn't want any of my children to come back to me years later and accuse me of dumping them in Africa because I didn't care. One of the main reasons I didn't believe this was a viable solution was the prevailing attitude towards children with special needs in Nigeria. Things have changed for the better since the boys were young, but sometimes old beliefs are hard to shift.

The new school year started, and David still didn't have a school. I had moved four miles away from my old home and was working nights—from 9:20 p.m. – 6:00 a.m. Jonathan's school was near my old house, so my younger brother, who lived with me, would take Jonathan to school, then go on to college. I would be home with David and would entertain him and try to keep him occupied until about noon. After his lunch, we would nap till about 2:30, then rush to pick Jonathan up from school. After my brother got home around 5:30, I would sleep until 8:00 p.m., have a shower, and rush to work. This would repeat the next day. And the day after. And the next day . . .

It didn't take long before it became clear I couldn't continue like that. I was always exhausted and didn't have the energy or will to do anything besides the established routine. My doctor diagnosed me with a mild case of clinical depression. They assigned David a social worker, who also facilitated Jonathan's transfer to a local school within five minutes of us. They found a special residential school for David in Hertfordshire; this was weekly boarding, so he'd be home every weekend. After a visit to the school, I was more agreeable to David going away than in the past. However, they wouldn't take him on as he was still in nappies. I was back to square one again.

A mother in the parent's support group suggested I visit my local Member of Parliament (MP) and ask him to help. I decided on a plan of action and made an appointment to see him. After Jonathan had gone to school, I went to my nearest constituency office. Before going in, I plied David with some Coca-Cola, which sent his energy levels into hyper drive. I went into the appointment with a "woe is me" apathetic, depressed demeanour, and let David do his thing. David did me proud; he was like the Tasmanian devil from the *Looney Tunes* cartoons, a whirlwind of energy. He scattered papers all over the place, spilled drinks, and wreaked havoc in that office; he just wouldn't sit still. All the while, I was half-heartedly trying to get him under control. I tearfully explained I would probably have to give up work as I was at the end of my tether, did not have a support network, and could no longer cope. Half an hour later, I left with an assurance that he would look into it. Two weeks later, the local authority offered us a place in the school in the neighbouring borough, including transport. I was so relieved; finally, we were getting somewhere.

At last, I was getting some sleep but still had many appointments I needed to go to in the daytime. These included parent/teacher coffee mornings at the school, Speech and Language Therapy (SALT) sessions, meetings with the social worker and the educational psychologist, Contact–A–Family support group meetings . . .. I didn't mind as I could handle things much better since I was getting more sleep.

David was still wearing nappies at five years old, and I became more and more concerned. In my support group, I saw sixteen-year-olds who were still in nappies and heard stories from parents struggling with their children smearing their faeces all over the wall—this was something I definitely didn't want. I spoke to the social worker, who informed me I was eligible for free disposable nappies because David was over the age of three. (I wasn't best pleased to discover I had needlessly spent money on nappies for the previous two years!) But apart from that, I didn't receive any advice or tips on how to move forward or deal with his toileting issues. Anytime we were home, I wouldn't put any nappies on David, but he just wouldn't go. He'd hold it in, and the minute I put a nappy on him, he would fill it. This frustrated me—its messy business changing a big, strapping, hyperactive five-year-old boy. I have since learned that David's toileting issues were probably linked to his sensory issues. I wish I'd known this at the time; I would have been more patient with him.

David was eventually toilet trained shortly after he turned six. I remember taking him to the bathroom in church one Sunday, and my friend Toks shrieked and hugged me when she saw us going in as she realised what this meant. It touched me deeply to have someone outside the family realise how big a deal it was to me, especially knowing not every autistic child achieves that milestone.

The twins were incredibly close—Jonathan was like David's shadow, and they often wanted to wear identical clothes (which I tried my best to discourage to no avail). They always wanted to play with the same toy and did everything together. I worried that going to different schools and being separated would be hard on them. My fears were unfounded; although they missed each other, they coped well. Jonathan thrived as he was no longer in the shadow of his more exuberant brother, and I could see their individual characters emerge clearly. David was the friendly, gregarious twin, while Jonathan was more serious, reserved, and chilled out. As they grew older, their roles reversed slightly. David seemed to understand that Jonathan was more aware of social cues and behaviours, so he would look to him as a role model and copy his behaviour. It was almost like Jonathan was his mirror to the world.

David was a very charming, social, likeable child, and our first social worker was an angel. She worked on putting together a package of respite care for the family, citing my diagnosis of depression as a valid reason. This all came together when David was about seven. It started with someone taking him out on a Saturday and Sunday every six weeks, giving me time to spend with Jonathan and run various errands.

He soon progressed to overnight stays, eventually alternating a Monday to Friday stay with a weekend stay every six weeks. David enjoyed his time away and was always happy to come back home. This was an absolute blessing to me and gave me a much-needed opportunity to recharge my batteries and spend uninterrupted quality time with Jonathan.

David had a rota of several support staff members, and it almost became a competition as to who would work with him; David had his favourites and was very popular with the staff. One of them, Angela, had lost a son around David's age and saw him as another son. Occasionally, she would ask my permission to take him to a social function, and I would agree. But the other staff weren't happy and reported her to the organisation she worked with. I told them she had my permission and blessing, and I always knew where he was. Another member of staff, TJ, was Deaf and used British Sign Language (BSL) to communicate, and he loved being with her. David was used to sign language and communicates with his own version of British Sign Language (BSL) because my sister Tina is Deaf and babysat him frequently. My mind was at rest; knowing my son was happy made me happy.

Unfortunately, the provision of these services is a postcode lottery. Each local authority area is autonomous and decides how to spend the money allocated to them by central government. I was fortunate to live in an affluent borough; I had friends who lived in other areas who couldn't get any respite. I knew a mother from the parent support group who had two autistic sons. She moved to another local authority area but moved back two years later, as she couldn't get the same level of support for her sons. The support I received was means-tested, and as my earnings were always just above the threshold to receive it for free, I had to make a financial contribution based on how much I earned. I didn't complain—I was just so grateful to receive any support at all.

It's vital for a parent's health and well-being to have a support network. I often felt too tired to attend parents' support meetings, but the benefits of going were crucial, and they also helped me to apply for disability benefit that I was unaware that David was eligible to receive. This helped to offset some of the additional financial costs incurred by having a child with special needs.

It's also crucial that siblings receive support. I know that I felt and continue to feel tremendous guilt that because I spent so much time and energy on David, which meant that Jonathan missed out a lot. I knew it was difficult for him—he didn't have that typical sibling relationship twins usually have and had to grow up quickly and behave responsibly from a young age. My local Contact-A-Family support group ran a project for siblings when Jonathan was about 12 or 13. These were invaluable; for the first time, he could talk about his experiences, thoughts and fears to people who understood exactly how he felt, without guilt or judgement. Contact-A-Family also organised trips, events, and social activities that the whole family could attend and enjoy without having to be constantly on the defensive, knowing that everyone there had a similar struggle.

I can't say enough about how my friendships have kept me sane. I don't have a huge number of friends, but I treasure the ones I have. Sandra would take Jonathan for weekends regularly, so he could spend time with her sons and another friend without worrying about David or me. This gave Jonathan the chance to interact with his peers and create a brotherly bond so strong, that the boys (or should I say young men) still consider themselves family, go on holidays together, and have served as each other's groomsmen at their weddings. Primrose would take both David and Jonathan for the day, so I could have some time for myself. Anthony, Peter, and Errol (my church brothers) would take David from me during church services, so I could enjoy the service in peace without being distracted by David.

The twins spent so much time with my friend Toks in the early years that I joked she had stolen Jonathan from me, as he really looked forward to going to see her. Their godfather, Stephen, and his brother Alex were always there to provide the male perspective; apart from my brothers, Axe and Kunle, they were the closest thing to a father to the twins. Edward from church would often take David out after church so I could relax and socialise with my friends. When Jonathan was a teenager, my pastor at the time, Marty Carnegie, took him out for lunch and gave him "the talk," setting the foundation for me to talk to him about girls, relationships, etc.

Vivienne - my "big little sister" - would talk to me for hours about anything and everything and share tips on the latest news or trends in autism that she'd discovered. She always remembered the boy's birthdays and would buy them little gifts. I appreciated this because their birthdays were so close to Christmas, so any presents they got were valued.

Louisa regularly hooked us up with free cinema tickets. Tracey and Paulette fought untold battles on my behalf that I was unaware of until years later. Tracey often babysat for me. (She ended up giving birth to an autistic child too). She'd tell me the boys were fine, and it wasn't a problem at all. Today, she's a passionate advocate for autistic children and children with additional needs. My sister-in-law, Toyin, babysat them so frequently, they were completely unaware that she was family by love and not by blood.

I am forever grateful to my Heavenly Father for the family he has blessed me with. They are a part of the village that broke down my naturally shy and reserved nature and helped me raise my children. Over the years, people have come into my life and been such a blessing to my family; I would need to write an entire book to tell everything they did to support me through the years.

Did You Know?

Sending Children "Back Home"

Sending children "back home" is a common phenomenon among African parents. Some parents do this for financial reasons. The cost of childcare in the UK is very high, and often it is more affordable to send the child to live with family in Africa and provide for their care and upkeep. However, the most common reason is to keep the children out of trouble and to ensure they become productive citizens. There are other reasons; I was encouraged to send one or both children to my parents to improve my prospects of having a second chance of building a (new) family.

It's usually boys—preteens to late teenagers—who are sent back, and this isn't regarded as an extreme response to an issue. It's viewed as a normal, beneficial step for them to encourage character building and instil positive attitudes in them. The most common age tends to be in the first couple of years of secondary school when they start to show early signs of juvenile or undesirable behaviour.

African parents tend to believe in discipline (corporal punishment) as a key tool in raising their children. In the United Kingdom, smacking or "beating" your child is illegal and is often viewed as a form of child abuse. Many parents believe this is why many of our youngsters are wayward; their parents aren't legally able to discipline when needed. However, "back home" in Africa, these restrictions don't apply. The general belief is that there is a better chance of achieving positive behavioural outcomes when children are brought up in their homeland of origin.

The outcomes? Mixed. For some, the shock of being in a different country, away from their friends, family, and everything they're accustomed to is enough to make them conform to a more acceptable way of behaviour. It's assumed they hope to return to their family sooner rather than later. However, others end up resenting their parents, especially if they undergo the strict parenting style often favoured in developing countries and end up estranged from their parents, sometimes rebelling against them.

The outcomes for children with special needs aren't clearly known, but the practice of sending children back to their parent's country of origin is not as prevalent as it used to be. Children tend to be more tech-savvy than their parents, more knowledgeable about their rights, and are more likely to know what to do if they find themselves stranded in their "motherland."

Additionally, safeguarding procedures are very rigorous since they've tightened up in recent years after a few high-profile child abuse/neglect cases. It would be very difficult to take a child to a different country to live without involving the authorities, and most parents would prefer less involvement with Social Care services, not more.

Helpful Hints

Building Your Tribe

As parents/guardians/carers, it's always important to have a network of people to support you in raising your children, but it's crucial when you have a child with any kind of additional support needs. If I—an introverted, proudly independent, and painfully shy woman—could build a tribe of people around me, anyone can! Here are my tips on how and why to build your tribe.

Who is your tribe?

Your family, friends, and supporters, along with anyone and everyone willing to join you and support you along your journey through life with your uniquely designed person.

What do they do?

They give you emotional, moral, spiritual, and practical support every step of the way on your journey through life. If anyone offers help, say, "Yes please," and "Thank you very much." In England, the Tesco advert says, "Every little helps" and it's so true. Help can range from babysitting your child with special needs or other children, assistance with shopping, housework, paperwork, and collecting children from school (or taking them to school). Some people may have connections with the education, health, housing, legal, or government systems and give you tips to better navigate them. Your tribe helps you with anything you need to make the journey a bit easier. Sometimes it's as simple as a five-minute adult conversation to keep you sane or a card celebrating a month with a dry bed. There is no "one size fits all" definition of what support you ask for or receive. It's what meets your needs. When I worked the night shift, my co-workers would cover for me so I could quickly go home (ten minutes there and back) to make sure my insomniac Houdini hadn't made a quick getaway while everyone was sleeping—this actually happened once!

Where do you find them?

The answer is anywhere and everywhere—at the school gates, in support meetings, at church, temple, or other places of worship, at work. When you go to your usual haunts, just keep your eyes and ears open to people who are willing to help. Don't allow pride or a sense of independence hinder you. You will always have an opportunity to pay it forward, and some people will become lifelong friends.

Why do you need a tribe?

You aren't Superman/Superwoman, and everyone needs a break. You need to be healthy, fit, and as rested as you can be to fight some of the battles you will inevitably fight to support your child. Another reason is because you're amazing and deserve a cheerleading squad behind you.

How do you build your tribe?

Part of your tribe will grow organically—friends, family, and loved ones who are naturally on your side and ready to support you. For others, you'll need to reach out to parent support groups, online forums, and connecting at events. Be brave! The more you do it, the easier it will become. Your tribe will celebrate your achievements, support you in the low times, and motivate you when you feel you can't go on. It's an amazing feeling when you know you have so many wonderful people who only want great things for your child; your journey becomes so much easier when you have people who understand what you're going through and are rooting for you and cheering you on.

CHAPTER 4

Why Isn't He Speaking?

The Search for a Way to Communicate

"What's wrong with David?"
"Why doesn't he talk?"
"Why does he talk funny?"

I've been asked questions like those above frequently over the years. And although I've come across many autistic children and adults whose speech characteristics are similar to David's, I've never met anyone quite like him.

Both twins had delayed speech, and I wasn't overly concerned about this because I'd learned that late language development was common among multiple births. However, as they approached their third birthday, Jonathan's speech took off, and he made up for lost time; he was such a chatterbox when he was young. The stark contrast between their speech and language development made me realise that something wasn't quite right with how David was developing—nothing else seemed particularly out of the ordinary until then.

Autism is often described as an invisible disability as it's not always noticeable that a person has autism until they speak. David is diagnosed as nonverbal, but I'm not comfortable with this description. Growing up, the primary marker of his autism had been his conspicuous lack of language and his atypical speech. Most people find David's speech unintelligible—sounds that make no sense. But I've found that people who have experience with deafness, autism, or special needs can understand his speech better.

It was David's delayed speech that led me to realise something was wrong. Both boys developed normally, albeit speaking later than their peers, with the usual words, such as mama, car, etc.; however, Jonathan was progressing much faster, and suddenly, David seemed to regress. He also started doing something I now know is called echolalia—repeating words spoken to him. If I said, "David, are you hungry?" his response would be, "You hungry."

David didn't point at things like a typical child. If he wanted something, he would grab my hand, take me to where the object was, throwing my hand in the direction of the location of the object. I didn't think too much of it; I just found it weird. I later found out this behaviour was typical to autistic children.

After receiving his diagnosis, he underwent extensive speech and language therapy. He started to talk more but was unable to articulate himself clearly. He was often frustrated, as it became clear that he could understand words but couldn't express himself. Fortunately, my sister Tina was an integral part of the twin's life in their early years. She is a British Sign language (BSL) user as she is profoundly deaf. They had a special bond—I think David identified with her, as he saw that they both have difficulties with speech. David started to communicate using basic BSL and gestures. From time to time, he still became distressed at his inability to express himself, but his behaviour improved vastly. Today, David communicates using a variety of methods—speech supported with basic BSL, fingerspelling (using the BSL manual alphabet), writing words on paper/typing on his tablet, and, to a lesser degree, a modified version of Picture Exchange Communication System (PECS).

My parents found it difficult to come to terms with David's diagnosis. They hadn't heard of autism, and the only thing they could see was that David couldn't speak. As the years went by, their constant question was, "Is he talking now?" I think it was harder for them than for me to accept David for who he is. I often felt that I had to shield them from the full details of how David's autism manifested.

The primary school David attended introduced us to PECS. The first phase would start during "circle time"—an informal, semi-structured social time used to develop children's emotional well-being. The teachers showed picture symbols representing a biscuit, fruit, orange juice, and blackcurrant juice and then asked the children to choose a picture from the food selection and another from the drink selection to indicate what they wanted. As the children became familiar with the process, they gradually added more pictures. Later on, at the beginning of the week, they would display a visual timetable for the week, using either a Velcro strip or magnetic pictures on a whiteboard. During unstructured playtime, the children were encouraged to choose the activities or games they wanted to play with. They used PECS to Makaton—a basic sign system based on BSL. Parents were usually offered a day's training course on Makaton and how to use it with their child. It aimed at reducing the pressure of using a spoken language, but at the same time, gave children tools to communicate. David's most popular Makaton signs were "biscuit" and "more."

By the time David moved on to secondary school, the PECS system had morphed into a little communication book David carried around with him. He would point at the pictures on different pages to get his message across. The book had pages dedicated to family, food, activities, routines, etc. He still has that book but rarely uses it now.

While he was still at secondary school, the teachers started to use "Social Stories™" (sometimes called Social Scripts) to communicate with the children. This prepared the children for upcoming events, let them know what to expect in certain situations, and taught them how to behave in certain social settings. For example, if they planned a trip to the seaside, the story would include details such as the day/date of the trip, who was going, the order of events, how they were getting there, the activities involved, and the journey back. This was very useful for David so he could be prepared for what was happening on the day. Social Stories can help prepare for events like trips to the doctor, the dentist, weddings, and holidays. Even now, I still write Social Stories to explain things to David. He brings his tablet to me and brings up his notes app if he wants me to write a Social Story about anything we're discussing. I think it helps him regulate his feelings and keep him calm about any upcoming events that might normally make him anxious.

To this day, David doesn't communicate in complete sentences. He also doesn't appear to understand how pronouns work—he thinks "you" refers to him (David), and "I" always refers to the other person in the conversation. People are often confused by how I speak to David, but I learned what worked for him by trial and error. For example, if I said, "Go upstairs to my room and get my bag," David would disappear upstairs. Twenty minutes later, I would go looking for him and find him standing at the top of the stairs, looking puzzled and not knowing what to do. So, I'd say, "Can David go to mummy's room and get mummy's bag from the bed please?" Then, he knew what room to go to, where to look, and could find my bag and bring it to me.

David has a few verbal stims—sounds he repeats over and over again. Recently, he has started articulating a new one: "Blobloblobloblo . . .." I feel terrible saying this, as I know he can't help himself, but it's something I haven't managed to get used to over the years, and it bothers me. It doesn't help that David has a really loud voice and doesn't seem to have a "volume register/regulator." He does try to lower his voice when I tell him he's too loud, but he genuinely seems to have difficulty maintaining a quiet sound. When I'm out with family and friends, they always tell me to leave him in peace when I try to ask him to lower his voice; and I feel bad for putting pressure on him to conform to society's expectations. But I see the looks; I hear the comments; I see people moving away from us; I feel the weight of judgments and attitudes from people who don't know us. And it breaks my heart when I see David notice it as well.

Unlike me, David is sociable, gregarious, and friendly. He likes to go up and say hello to people; he enjoys being a part of things. So, when we go out, even to places with people we know, I'm always on alert, like a helicopter mum, trying to make sure David doesn't cross boundaries or offend people. It's not right, and it's not fair on David, myself, or our friends. But I'm always worried that we will outstay our welcome, and people will get fed up. Maybe I'm paranoid, but I know I've been excluded from invitations because of David, and some places have made us feel unwelcome.

Wonderfully Complex

Over the years, I've realised that I've fallen into the trap of thinking speech equals communication and hadn't understood that David had been communicating all along. So, what is communication? What does it involve? It's not just speaking and listening, reading and writing. There's so much more involved. We talk about verbal and nonverbal communication, and we think about speech, gestures, and body language. Oftentimes, the speech of autistic children is disordered. Some children have limited speech and not much vocabulary, while others may have an extensive vocabulary, but specific areas of interest they will talk about endlessly—not conversing, but talking at others. Many autistic children find it difficult to understand the tone and inflections of the voice. They may have problems understanding the meaning of words and sentences and tend to understand things in a literal fashion. They may use repetitive or rigid language, often repeating what they hear (echolalia) or saying the same things over and over. They also tend to have poor nonverbal skills.

When we think about non-verbal communication in autistic children, we usually think about facial expressions, gestures, sign language/sign systems, and body language. We don't always consider the behaviours they display as communication. However, stimming, meltdowns, and self-injurious behaviours are ways in which autistic children and adults express how they feel.

Many times, what we would describe as challenging behaviour occurs because the autistic child or person is frustrated at their inability to communicate their needs to others. I believe if we view behaviour as a function of communication, we will be better placed to start understanding our autistic loved ones better. Over the years, I've had to learn the driving factor behind David's behaviour in order to support him and try and meet his needs. I don't always get it right, but I understand him a lot better than I used to, and I believe he feels comfortable being himself when he is with me.

E – Escape (from difficult tasks, unpleasant or stressful situations)

David has had meltdowns and engaged in self-injurious behaviour when he felt overwhelmed, extremely distressed, anxious, or fearful. Giving him a way to communicate his motions helps prevent or de-escalate them. David now has better control over his outbursts and will say "breathe in", then count four breaths in and out to help regulate his emotions. I breathe along with him; it seems to help him, and it also allows me to stay calm in those situations. Even during these uncertain times (during COVID-19) of changing regulations and not knowing what's permitted from day to day, David tells me, "Calm. Breathe in." He doesn't do it perfectly; he breathes in fast and counts to four, then releases his breath quickly. But just performing the action helps him focus on calming down.

A – Attention

Sometimes, the behaviours David displays are a ploy to get my attention. Anytime I talk to Jonathan for any length of time, he starts vocalising loudly or bothering me to get my attention focused solely on him. I try my best to ensure that I give David a lot of attention when his brother is around—it's difficult because I don't see as much of Jonathan as I used to. I also encourage David to get my attention in an appropriate way, asking him to tell me if he wants something from me. Including him in our conversation helps, but it means I don't get a lot of one-on-one time with Jonathan. This doesn't usually happen when I'm talking to other people; on reflection, I think there's an element of jealousy at play. He can't converse with Jonathan or me as easily as we can with each other, and we are the closest people to him.

T' – Tangibles (desired items or activities)

This is behaviour aimed at getting something or access to an activity. David is fiercely independent and strives to do as much as he can on his terms. When he was younger, he found it difficult to ask for the things he needed and got frustrated when he couldn't get what he wanted or couldn't achieve what he was trying to. Then the crying, screaming, slapping his face with both hands, and occasionally punching his face started. I would need to give him time and space to calm down and find out what he wanted by process of elimination—asking him questions one by one:

"Does David want orange juice?"

"No? Does David want some biscuits?"

I continued asking questions until we identified what he wanted.

Nowadays, David is proactive and will ask for his needs unprompted. He even accepts and asks for help—sometimes. This is a huge achievement for a perfectionist who used to resist any assistance.

S – Sensory

This is behaviour that fulfils a need for sensory input. Many (if not all) autistic children indulge in stimming (self-stimulating behaviour such as rocking, humming, flicking fingers, spinning, walking on tiptoes, biting their nails, chewing their lips, cracking their knuckles repeatedly, or twitching a leg). But the DSM-5 includes stimming as part of the criteria in an autism diagnosis and defines it as "stereotyped or repetitive motor movements, use of objects and speech." Stimming is not necessarily bad unless it's a form of self-injurious behaviour, such as head banging, punching, or biting. Stimming sometimes occurs as a way to regulate sensory input, (e.g., blocking out excess overstimulation or providing extra sensory input when under-stimulated). It can also help manage emotions, cause pleasurable feelings (by releasing endorphins), and be a way to self-soothe.

I must confess, I used to try and get David to either stop stimming or reduce the intensity of his stimming. I felt every stare—real or imagined—and internalised every ignorant comment. I judged myself as a bad mother, feeling bad that I couldn't protect my son from people's prejudices, feeling irritated by his actions, and simultaneously feeling enormous guilt for entertaining such feelings. Now, when we're at home, I leave him to stim to his heart's content, only intervening if his verbal stims become too noisy and asking him to lower his voice.

Sometimes, I think back to the early days of David's diagnosis and remember the doctor's words—David would need institutional care all his life. He made me feel like my son would never amount to anything, that he'd never achieve much in his life. David doesn't have any qualifications education-wise, and people don't see him as someone who will contribute anything worthwhile to society. But everyone who comes into close contact with him is touched by him. He has a huge heart and loves connecting with people in his own way. He is much friendlier than his brother or I and has taught me to be brave; to stand up and speak out when I'd prefer not to; to look out for the needs of those who are unable to speak for themselves when I'd rather stay quiet and comfortable in my corner. I believe he has made me a better person, a more compassionate human being, less judgmental of others. Despite the struggles, heartache, and barriers, I believe that David has a purpose on this earth. I don't fully understand what and why, but my job is to love him, support him, and help him flourish, and I will do my best to *do that as his mother.*

Did You Know?

Augmentative and Alternative Communication

These are some of the techniques and resources that autistic children and young people can use to help them communicate with others:

- Makaton/Sign languages-- forms of communication which help relieve the pressure to speak while giving autistic children and adults a way to communicate.
- Picture Exchange Communication System (PECS)—use of symbols and pictures to help with communication between an autistic person and their caregiver. This can be adapted to suit the individual needs of autistic children.
- Communication boards—used to show things like diaries and schedules of events to help prepare for the days ahead.
- Communication books—can help with one-to-one communication. They can be used in a variety of ways; from showing an image to request something they want, to a sequence of images to ask for a desired outcome.
- Social Stories™—used to help prepare for specific events. They can be read repetitively to reinforce the message. These can be bought, or you can be trained to write your own Social Stories.
- Communication devices and apps—several apps that can be downloaded to tablets to help facilitate communication. Pragmatic Organisation Dynamic Display (PODD) is one of the more popular ones. PODD's are usually custom-made for the person who needs them. They also come in book format.

Helpful Hints

Effective Communication

Always address them by name when you speak to them, so they know you are talking to them.

Remember the acronym KISS when communicating with your autistic child- Keep It Short and Simple. Don't overload them with too many words as it may confuse them.

Speak slowly in short sentences. Pause between sentences to give them time to process.

Be specific. Tell them exactly what you want of them

Be clear—don't use vague or figurative language; autistic children (and adults) are very literal in their understanding of language.

Don't ask open-ended questions; ask questions that include a choice.

Make sure the environment is conducive to communication; if you're in a crowded or noisy environment, they may find it difficult to concentrate.

Give feedback; reward their attempts to communicate. Reinforce communication with praise and positive comments.

Give your child a reason to communicate – provide a high interest object, or a toy/game that's difficult to operate.

Use communication aids (visual supports, gestures, PECS, Sign Language etc).

Consider your child's personality, preferred communication styles, habits, and mood when trying to communicate with them.

Remember; your child's behaviour is a form of communication.

Be patient. It will take time and hard work to build up your child's communication skills, but it's well worth the effort.

CHAPTER 5

There's Nothing Wrong with Him; He's Just Naughty

Black and Autistic—Double Discrimination

Being black, male, and British is complicated. Add in the extra factor of being autistic, and it brings a whole range of issues that you wouldn't begin to appreciate if you're not in that position. Diagnosis of autistic children from minority ethnic backgrounds has traditionally been low, even though autism is no respecter of race, culture, or socioeconomic groups. It's only in recent years that the level of diagnosis has risen. Even with a diagnosis, Black Asian and Minority Ethnic (BAME) communities tend not to access services to support their children; this can be due to several reasons.

I believe the biggest reason is denial. The awareness of autism in BAME communities is improving, but it's often perceived as a "western illness." Cultural beliefs surrounding disability means that many parents struggle to accept a diagnosis because of the stigma, blame, and shame associated with it. The Black community tends to be religious and consequently, generally doesn't accept the fact that there's no cure. Many community languages don't have an equivalent word for autism, and it's often considered to be a mental health condition (madness) or a curse. The odd behaviour would be labelled as being naughty, lacking discipline, or in the case of boys, typical boisterous male behaviour. Once the community becomes aware of the diagnosis, the family tends to isolate themselves, and stop attending functions or church/mosque/temple because of the shame and stigma. I remember a friend telling me how she found out she had a cousin with special needs after attending a family celebration at her uncle's house. She saw a boy around thirteen or fourteen years old who she hadn't seen before coming downstairs to get a drink from the fridge. She asked her cousin who the boy was and got the reply, "He's, my brother."

People always commented to me how I took David everywhere with me. My response was usually, "What am I supposed to do with him?" I realised later that I was expected to hide him away, out of shame or embarrassment about his "condition."

The culmination of cultural and religious beliefs leads to parents shouldering all the caring responsibilities for their children—not washing their dirty linen in public. This is one reason why the uptake of services to support autistic children is quite low in these communities compared to the public. However, the attitudes of professionals across the board to families of autistic children don't help.

It starts in schools; teachers don't believe a child (particularly black boys) might have a condition, even on the occasions where they do have a diagnosis and/or an Individual Education

Plan/Education and Health Passport (IEP/ EHP). They are quick to label the child as naughty, disruptive, or acting out because of bad parenting. Statistics[10] show that a quarter of black autistic children are excluded from the school system—double discrimination of sorts. It's universally accepted that early intervention is crucial to ensure positive outcomes for autistic children. The delay in receiving a diagnosis is twofold; from the parent's end, the denial to admit that there is something different about the child, and the school's resistance in accepting there's something going on with the child.

When it comes to receiving a diagnosis, there seems to be a reluctance with professionals to accept that any difficulties a child is experiencing could be due to an underlying condition. In my experience, and based on what I've heard from other parents, there's a tendency to blame the parents, home environment, or even the child.

I had a university degree when I had my twins, but I felt a lot of the social care and health professionals were quite dismissive of me in our interactions and didn't listen to what I had to say. At the time, I felt this was because I looked much younger than my age. However, looking back, I feel it was possibly also because I was a black single mother, and all their biases were coming into play. Black people can be passionate, especially when trying to get support for their children, and this can come across as aggression. This leads to labels such as difficult, stubborn, uncooperative, resistant, antagonist, troublemaker, etc., being bandied around. Overall, the relationship between professionals and BAME parents of autistic children is strained. Parents seem to be suspicious of the professionals, while the professionals tend to see parents as antagonistic or confrontational. I am an introvert by nature, and I'm used to being invisible and unheard. I have found it quite challenging to stand up to the powers that be, to advocate for David's needs and wants. I'm a people pleaser and don't like drawing attention to myself or making waves. On the few occasions I've made a stand, I've been made to feel like an angry black woman, which is far from who I am!

As much as I feel the odds are stacked against David—being a young, autistic, black man—I am grateful I live in the UK. Awareness of autism is fairly good; the issue is knowing how to interact with autistic individuals. Racism is a fact of life, and there are issues around privilege, injustice, and unconscious bias everywhere in the world. But the last time David went on holiday (October 2017), my worst fears were realised, and my heart was shattered.

David looks forward to his holidays and travels every year, usually with someone else from his home and two members of staff, usually one male and one female or two males. For the previous three years, the same male staff member went with him, but on this occasion, two females who hadn't been away with him before accompanied him. I was aware the regular male wasn't going but was under the impression that another male who'd travelled with him before was going.

His holiday was in Spain, and he left on Thursday to return on Monday. On Friday evening, the manager of his home called me.

"Hi Tayo, how are you? First of all, I just want to say we've sorted everything, and David is OK."

Straightaway, my heart sank, and I began to panic—a thousand thoughts of what might have happened flood my brain. "What happened?"

"You know how David gets excited? Well, they were coming down to lunch in the hotel. They were in the lift, and David was getting happy, saying, 'Lunch, lunch!'"

"O—kay . . .."

"Well, the other people in the lift started looking at him funny and moving away from him. David got agitated and started hitting himself. People started to panic and tried to get out of the lift, and he hit a lady's glasses off her face in the middle of his behaviour. When they got out, they called the police, who arrested David."

I started shaking, and my phone was wet with tears. "What?"

She explained the police saw David as an aggressive black man with mental health issues and had arrested him on the grounds of threatening behaviour. The support workers tried to explain he was autistic and had a learning disability, but a perfect storm of culture clash, language barriers, and pressure from the hotel staff meant nobody listened to them. A couple of hours later, they managed to get a doctor from the hospital to examine him; the doctor confirmed that David wasn't aggressive. It was just a misunderstanding caused by his autistic behaviour. He was released without charge. Throughout the whole incident, David was subdued but kept on repeating "lunch, lunch." He hadn't been fed and was hungry.

The hotel refused to allow David back, and the support workers had to pay for another hotel; the holiday continued without further incident. But I was devastated by the thought that David had been arrested and detained in a police cell. I can't help thinking that things would have panned out differently if he wasn't Black. I kept on thinking, what would've happened if David had resisted the arrest or lashed out? Would he have ended up as another statistic of a black man languishing in a foreign prison, or even worse, a statistic of police brutality?

Of course, David told the staff, "No tell mummy." He didn't want me to know; he thought he'd be in trouble and wouldn't be allowed to go on holiday. The first thing he said to me on his return (after plying me with gifts) was, "Holiday good. David good time!"

Obviously, I quickly told him that I knew all about his misadventure, and I wasn't happy with him.

David hasn't been abroad since. The premiums on the holiday insurance, where they can find it, have been exorbitant. I remind David that he can't go on holiday if he doesn't behave, but I feel terrible because I know he wasn't trying to be difficult—it was just the way he expresses himself.

Did You Know?

Systemic Racism in the United Kingdom

Many young Black pupils in the school system in the UK experience racism as a fact of everyday life.

The impact of racist behaviours and attitudes on young Black people permeates through every aspect of their lives and being.

Institutional or systemic racism is experienced by Black people in the following areas: education, employment, health, crime, and finance.

The findings of a report published by the Young Men's Christian Association[7] (YMCA) in October 2020 shows:

- **95**% of Black people experience racism in school and work.

- 54% feel the colour of their skin hinders their employment prospects.

- 64% worry about their treatment by the police.

- Black pupils are three times more likely to be permanently excluded from school compared to their White peers. This is possibly due to the negative preconceptions held by their teachers.

- Black pupils feel that 50% of their barriers to academic achievement are due to the false perceptions of their teachers.

- 54% of Black people experienced bias at the recruitment stage of employment, particularly when they have non-white names.

- 54% face prejudice from their employer.

- 52% feel there is a lack of diversity in leadership roles.
- 50% feel there is a lack of diversity in the workplace.
- 47% feel there is a lack of opportunities for progression.
- 54% feel they need to police themselves, so they do not conform to stereotypes.
- 55% worry about being falsely accused of a crime.
- 54% do not trust the police.
- In mental health services, Black male patients are more likely to be viewed as aggressive and are more likely to be sectioned (admitted and detained in a hospital without their consent).
- There is anecdotal evidence of Black people being denied medication because of the false belief that they have a high tolerance of pain.
- Black people report Mental Health professionals disregard their health concerns.
- Black women are more likely to have experienced a mental health disorder such as anxiety or depression in the past week.
- Black men are most likely to have suffered a psychotic disorder in the last year.
- Cabinet Office Race Disparity Audit found that racism has a damaging effect on young Black people's mental health.

Helpful Hints

How to Make a Difference

As people of colour, the truth is we have to be the change that we want to see. The key word is education. We need to educate people about what we go through and what support we need. However, this is going to be a long journey, with no quick fixes.

- Educate your family
- Educate your community
- Educate your church
- Join a support group, such as:
    - Abigail Outreach Ministry
    - Contact-A-Family
    - National Autistic Society
- Accept help from your friends and family. There's nothing to gain from being proud.
- Don't be afraid to ask for help when you need it. You have nothing to lose; they can only say no, and they might say yes.
- Take advantage of respite care from your local authority.
- Find a sibling group for your other child(ren) to get support from.

CHAPTER 6

Oh No! He's Eloped

Wanderlust

The first time I heard the term elopement regarding autistic children, I thought it was ridiculous. An eight-year-old boy eloping? Who is he getting married to? It sounded like the stuff of a *Twilight Zone* episode! However, I learned it's a term used to describe the behaviour of vulnerable people who wander or run away from their homes/schools/institutions. David was my little Houdini, an escape artist extraordinaire. I'm convinced his little escapades contributed to the grey hairs I started amassing at an early age (in my thirties).

David started wandering off at a very young age. I remember his first escapade clearly. At the time, I was working nights at the post office, and Jonathan was in school. I'd stayed awake as long as I could after dropping Jonathan off—it was just David and me at home. I dozed off on the sofa, and the next thing I knew, there was a loud banging on the door. I got up, dazed and confused, to find the owner of the corner shop, with David by his side. He was only four years old at the time.

I later discovered how he'd managed to escape. I couldn't lock the door from the inside with a key, so I'd bolted the door at the bottom and top and used the Chubb lock to lock it from the inside. There was a narrow corridor from the front door to the living room. David had unbolted the bottom lock, used his legs to support himself on both sides of the corridor walls, and manoeuvred himself up, unbolted the top bolts, unlocked the door, and used his body weight to swing the door open and run out. It was jaw-dropping to behold; he did it almost in one movement. As a direct result of this incident, I installed a combination lock on the door. Unfortunately, David excelled at working out the combination, so I had to change the combination frequently!

If you have any interaction with autistic individuals, you will be familiar with the fact that they don't seem to need much sleep. I worked nights for a large part of the early years raising my children, so a few incidents happened at night. I recall arriving home around 6:30 a.m. to find David sitting at the bottom of the stairs with empty crisp packets strewn around him. But even more alarming was the morning I arrived home to find the front door wide open. I rushed upstairs to the twins' room, and just as I feared, David's bed was empty. I woke my brother and shouted at him, asking where David was. He was still groggy and disoriented, so I didn't wait for an answer. I raced out of the house, jumped in my car, and started driving to Asda (the U.K. version of Walmart). At the time, David was obsessed with Asda. I spotted him about to cross the main road at the traffic lights about 7–8 minutes away from home. I pulled up, opened the passenger door, and told him to get in. I was so scared—anything could have happened. I have found David in Asda on a number of occasions when he's disappeared from home—the local Asda is about a fifteen-minute walk from our home.

I learned over the years the importance of being vigilant around David, but even being hyperaware and super vigilant doesn't always prevent these escapades from happening. When David was about eight or nine years old, we went on a family outing to a park with some friends; it was a huge park on the other side of London, so I was on high alert. These were not familiar surroundings, so I was keen to make sure David was always with me. I kept a firm grip on David, and the day was going so well, until…

I looked down to say something to David and realised the cunning little fox had wormed his way out of my grasp and done a runner! I was beside myself with worry. Nobody had a clue how long he'd been gone. We immediately split up into search groups, and some people went outside the park to search for him. It seemed like an eternity, but I believe it was 10–15 minutes later, one of my friends called me to say they'd found him. He was on the platform of the tube (underground train station), jumping in and out of the train carriages as they stopped on the platform. We left the park soon afterwards, as I was scared it would happen again, and this time we might not find him. Those were truly scary times. I couldn't keep him cooped up at home—he had far too much energy to burn, and we'd all go stir-crazy sitting at home. But I was constantly worried about his safety. I couldn't take my eyes off him, but I had another child to take care of and tasks to complete—and it was only me. I felt I was losing at life and motherhood. No matter how hard I tried, it was never good enough. I thought I always had to explain or justify David's behaviour, and how I responded or dealt with it. It was never-ending and extremely stressful.

I have always struggled with believing I'm a good mother, largely due to the issues I faced with David. But the fact is, David hasn't only escaped from my care; he has absconded from various settings with different individuals and organisations. I remember a particular incident in his primary school. It was well known that David was skilled at using his gymnastic abilities to climb, swing, and manoeuvre locks (not with keys) and combination codes to get out of rooms—have I mentioned that he was extremely hyperactive as a child? He would regularly get into the playground and jump on a member of staff's soft-top (convertible car). One day, I was told that he'd managed to get out of the school's premises but was found quickly. However, a year later, I heard the full story of what transpired on that day.

I was attending evening classes to learn British Sign Language, and one evening, our tutor was ill. Our class was merged with another sign language class. We did introductions in sign language—names, occupations, family. One student said they taught in a special school for autism. So, I responded, saying I had an autistic son who went to school in Fulham. He asked the name of the school, and lo and behold, it was the same school. I asked if he knew David, and the whole story came out. David had made his way into the playground, jumping on the car as usual, and noticed someone had left the gate open. He made his escape, ran out onto the street, made his way on Fulham Bridge Road, and ran across Fulham Bridge. He was quite fast, and the staff couldn't keep up with him. The police were called, and it was the police helicopters that spotted him as he made a run for it across the bridge. I think the school was afraid of being sued, which is why I received an abridged version of the incident.

Looking back over the years, I'm amazed that David is still alive today. As a Christian, at times, I imagine that David has an overworked, highly qualified, elite guardian angel allocated to him. I have read Frank Peretti's books *This Present Darkness*[8] and *Piercing the Darkness*[9]; his descriptions of the warrior angels assigned to protect the beleaguered pastor comfort and resonate with me. The first incident that made me realise the high level of risk associated with David was immediately after a church service when he was about five years old. This was due to the gate being left open (I sense a theme here); David dashed straight out of the church, through the parking area, and across the road into the path of an oncoming car. He was knocked down, an ambulance was called, and he was rushed to the hospital. Fortunately, the car wasn't going fast, and he only suffered a concussion. He was kept overnight for observation. The incident petrified me – I thought he was going to die. I think that was the first time my friends understood why I was always anxious around David and hovered around him so much when we were out. That fear has diminished with time, but it has never left me.

Over the years, Social Services (the UK equivalent of Child Protective Services) has attempted to put David on the child protection register, citing that he's a danger to himself. I have always resisted this as the child protection register is perceived as being for children who have been abused or at risk of abuse. As a black woman, I worried about the negative connotations and inferences that would be made about me. The day I met David's new social worker was memorable for all the wrong reasons. It was May 1, 1997. I remember the date because it was the day the UK elected Tony Blair as Prime Minister. David's school was closed because it was a polling station, and I was on a training course on the early shift at Royal Mail. I came home about 1 p.m., and my younger brother told me David was missing and the police wanted to speak to me (this was pre-mobile/cell phones). I thought he was joking at first, but he assured me that David had gotten away from him as he took Jonathan to school.

I went to the police station and answered a lot of questions. They asked where he'd be likely to go. They also advised me they couldn't allocate much manpower to the search, as they were busy with election duties, and suggested I look for him myself. Looking back on it now, that excuse was outrageous (and possibly racist), but at the time, I wasn't thinking straight and was worried about what could have happened to him. It was an extremely hot day, and I was worn out from the training session and extremely anxious. I walked the streets of Battersea, searching for David, and periodically returned home to see if there was any news. My mind was all over the place; I imagined him being involved in a car accident, critically injured, or even worse, dead. Finally, at around 3:00 p.m., I went home. My brother greeted me with news of David being found, and I needed to go to a police station in the neighbouring local authority to pick him up.

David had been found about twenty minutes after he absconded from my brother. But because I live on the border of two local authority areas, they hadn't been able to identify who I was and find me. I arrived at the police station to a cheerful David, eating chips with tomato sauce. However, his new social worker was also there and disapprovingly interrogated me about how David had managed to escape from my care. Needless to say, my relationship with this social worker didn't recover.

The incident that scared me the most happened abroad when the boys were about eight years old. We had gone on a day trip to Le Touquet in France. It was an organised trip, and a few of my friends had gone as well; Shanita, with her children Adunni, Ariyo, and Shade, and my friends Folusho and Baba. We'd had a lovely day on the beach—Jonathan was having a great time with his playmates, and I was focussing on David. We played on the beach, but I didn't let him get near the water. Have I told you that David loves anything to do with water? He's a strong swimmer and loves doing the dishes!

So, we'd had a great day and were packing up, ready to go on the coach for the trip home, and David made a break for it, running towards the sea. I ran after him. Unfortunately, I'm not a runner and was struggling in the sand. Instead of getting closer to David, the distance between us was growing—then he disappeared! It felt like it was happening in slow motion. My heart sank, my heart was pounding in my chest, and I felt like I was about to faint. I have never been so frightened in my life. So many thoughts rushed through my mind simultaneously—I'd have to send Jonathan home with my friends, find a hotel to stay the night . . . where was the nearest police station? I didn't speak French. What would I tell my family? I felt like such a bad mother. I didn't even know I was crying. I felt crippled by fear.

My friends rallied around me, and everyone joined in the search. We found him about twenty minutes later, sitting on the coach. I was weak with relief—I couldn't even tell him off; I was so happy to see him!

Our autistic children tend to keep us on our toes. David's boarding school had to revamp its security system because of him. They had been using combination locks on all their doors but had to keep changing them as David kept working out the combinations. Eventually, they changed to an old-fashioned lock-and-key system, and staff had to always keep their keys on them. At times, when I'd collect David from respite care, he would open the combination lock to let us out when they took too long to sign us out. Even now, when I pick David up for the weekend, he goes straight to the safe, punches in the code, and retrieves his wallet if the staff are taking too long going through the signing out process. I'm just grateful he's honest.

I look back and remember his lock-breaking tendencies from an early age. He figured out (broke!) the fridge lock within a couple of weeks of us getting it—he was only four years old at the time! And as for stairgates, he just climbed over them. This meant having stairgates were more dangerous than coping without them. David is thirty now and is a lot more settled. The last wandering incident I recall was about three years ago; Jonathan had picked him up and brought him home for the weekend. Apparently, as soon as they got in, David said, "Shoes, shoes," indicating that he'd forgotten to bring his shoes. Jonathan went upstairs to use the loo and heard the front door bang shut. He rushed downstairs, and David had disappeared. In a panic, Jonathan rushed out and drove around looking for his brother. He found him at the bus stop, waiting for the bus to take him back to his residential home.

There are so many more incidents I could tell you—he's run from a wedding reception, from a family-friendly stag do, from theme parks, from his support workers. He's even managed to get off his school bus and turn up in his brother's primary school! But these are the more memorable events.

Did You Know?

Elopement

What is Elopement?

Elopement is a term used to describe an individual with autism or cognitive challenges who wanders or runs away from a caregiving facility or environment. It's an extremely common phenomenon, with about 50% of autistic children aged 4–10 years old. It may continue into adult life.

Breakdown of incidents:

- Two-thirds involve close call traffic incidents
- Police are involved in one-third of incidents
- Near drownings account for one-third of incidents

Why do autistic children Elope?

- The sheer enjoyment of feeling free.
- They just want to go somewhere they enjoy.
- They want to escape an anxious situation.
- They are trying to get away from sensory stimuli.
- They want to explore a place of interest.

Helpful Hints

What To Do if Your Child Wanders

Be alert.
    Secure your home.
    Teach your children alternative behaviour (if you can).
    Alert your neighbours.
    Create a family emergency plan.
    Maintain an emergency form for your neighbours and safety personnel (police, etc.).
    Consider getting a tracking device.
    Get an ID bracelet or other ID device for your child to wear, so you can be alerted once he is found.

CHAPTER 7

Puberty and the Hormone Express

Puberty: that wonderful time that marks the transition from childhood to adulthood. This was the most challenging time I've ever experienced—I'm glad it's over! David had started secondary school, and even though he was labelled non-verbal, he is also high functioning. He went to school for children with moderate learning difficulties, which had a unit for autistic children. After some discussions with David's class teacher and head teacher, we identified and agreed on the schools we thought were suitable. The head teacher contacted the schools, arranged for David to be observed in the classroom by his prospective teachers, and arranged the admission process between them. I allowed myself to be guided by them and let them take the lead because I was overwhelmed with finding Jonathan a school, which was far more stressful and complicated. I know not everyone has such a smooth process.

I attended several events at Jonathan's school to explain the process and advising parents on the next steps. I arranged for him to take entrance exams and visited various open days. The competition for schools in my local government area was tight, and there were a greater number of children in his year group than usual. Jonathan eventually got into his third-choice school (it wasn't one of my choices).

There were about six children in David's class, but he was the only one who didn't "speak." David, like most autistic children, was resistant to change, and he struggled; I feel he felt the difference between himself and other children keenly. Leaving the familiarity of his primary school, where he'd been for six years, and moving to this big school, where he didn't know anyone, was hard on him. I'd tried to prepare him by visiting the school with him a few times before moving. I'd bought both Jonathan and David's new uniforms and school supplies, stressing it was a good thing that they were both moving on to big school and tried to make it fun and exciting. It seemed to work for a bit, but it was difficult for the whole family.

We settled into our new routine muddled our way through, and puberty hit with a vengeance! Jonathan wasn't a talkative child at the best of times, and he just withdrew into himself and became this nonverbal, grunting creature. David, who had always been a cheerful child, just became louder and escalated his self-injurious behaviour. As a young teen, he went through a brief season of banging his head on the wall when he was frustrated. Thankfully, this didn't last long, but he moved onto slapping himself in the face with both hands. As if this wasn't distressing enough, he moved on to punching himself in the face and screaming (have I mentioned that David has a very loud voice and doesn't seem to know how loud he is or how to regulate his volume?).

Jonathan started becoming more independent, going out with his friends, going on more sleepovers at my friend Sandra and her sons' place. The differences between the boys, their behaviours, lifestyles, and abilities became glaringly obvious, and David didn't take it well. He could see Jonathan go out by himself, but he was always stuck with me, which really annoyed him. I started leaving places earlier than planned because of David's behaviour and eventually stopped going out. I'd drop Jonathan off at places and ask my friends to bring him back. I stopped having people over as sometimes they'd complain about David's behaviour; I would think to myself - *this is his home! Where else could he be himself?* I'm naturally an introvert, so this gave me an excuse not to go out. I become more guarded and closed in, and to this day, I rarely entertain people at home. Only family and very close friends come over.

I never really considered the impact of having an autistic child in the family but looking back on my experiences and other families I know, it was enormous. For me, it became noticeable in the teenage years, when David's behaviour escalated.

Work:

I was a postwoman for fifteen years, and this was purely because of the convenience of shift work. I worked mainly nights and early shifts so I could balance my work with my caring responsibilities. Many families of autistic children, especially single-parent families, tend to give up work—the constant appointments with various professionals, meetings at school, or calls to pick up your child because he is acting out means employers quickly lose their patience and label you as unreliable. Our appointments with the speech therapist were during office work hours, and the social service meetings, educational and clinical psychologist appointments were also during the daytime. Because I worked nights, I was able to attend all our appointments, but this meant that I was constantly sleep deprived, and didn't have energy for normal everyday life.

Relationships:

I was on my own from day one and knew I had to be strong, self-sufficient, and do everything in my power to advocate for David. But I have seen marriages and relationships break down under the pressure of caring for an autistic child. I tended to see (and yes, this is a broad generalisation) the following sequence of events: The couple/family received the diagnosis of autism. After the initial shock wore off, one parent (usually, but not always mum) did her best to get to grips with the situation and tried to find out what the next steps were. The other parent (dad) and other friends and family remained in denial and refused to accept the child is different. Mum begins feeling she has no support and is doing everything on her own. Dad feels shut out, helpless, and sometimes resentful. Eventually, the relationship breaks down under the stress of dealing with all the issues surrounding raising a child with autism. Anecdotal evidence has stated the prevalence of divorce is 80% where there is a child with autism, but nobody seems to know where this figure has come from[10]. However, a study carried out in 2010 found that the incidence of divorce was only 10% greater than couples who didn't have autistic .[11]

In my experience, I've only met three couples with an autistic child who were still together (and I've met a lot of families). It's largely the mothers who take on the responsibilities of dealing with the challenges of bringing up children with autism. But I have met some dads who are doing an awesome job as well.

I haven't personally seen any examples of a mother of an autistic child dating successfully, but I would love to be disabused of my impression that it simply doesn't happen. My experience of dating has been unfortunate. When the boys were younger, I didn't have the energy to even contemplate entering a relationship. As they grew older, during their primary school years, men started to show an interest in me but would backtrack once they realised I was a single mother. Those who weren't deterred by this soon vanished when they realised that one of my children had special needs. As time went on, the men who approached me made it clear what they were interested in; one man commented that I should be grateful for any attention I received as I was damaged goods! As much as I'd like to share my life with someone, I've made peace with the fact that I'm on my own for the foreseeable future.

Social Life:

I quickly found out who my real friends were. I've tried not to be too hard on those who didn't stick around; it's a lot to deal with, and it's not easy. People have their own issues they're dealing with and can't always handle all the drama that goes with autism in a family. Every minute and detail have to be planned for social gatherings, with contingencies made if things don't go to plan. Not everyone can cope with this.

An example: When the boys were about 10 years old, we went to a restaurant -Noodle House - with a group of friends and their children, and David started flapping, fidgeting, and making noise because the food was taking too long. People began to stare, shake their heads disapprovingly, and mutter in our general direction. I touched David on his shoulder. "Five minutes. The food will be here soon."

The waiters brought the plates over, but David's meal still hadn't arrived. Then, the screaming and hitting his face with both hands started. I got up, quickly chatted to the designated support friend for that evening and asked them to bring Jonathan home after the meal. I gathered my bags and took David home, feeling multiple eyes boring into my back as we left. I kept imagining the comments from the other people in the restaurant;

"That child needs a good beating."

"What kind of mother is she?"

"Why would she even bring him here?"

"Finally, thank God they're leaving."

I finished my walk of shame out of the restaurant and drove home, feeling humiliated, inadequate, and exhausted. This scenario played out in church, family gatherings, barbecues, picnics, trips out . . .. Slowly, the invitations dwindled. Some people would invite just Jonathan, and I was grateful for this. Others just quietly disappeared from my life. But others made an effort to include me. And some would babysit both boys for me if I needed to get out (thank you, Toks, Primrose, and Tracey). Some would take both boys out for a couple of hours so I could catch up with my friends (Peter, Puraseni, Alex, Anthony, Errol—I'm so grateful). And there was one person who made it his mission to periodically take David off my hands to give me breathing space (Edward, you're my hero!).

Holidays:

I was one of those brave parents who went on holiday regularly with my children. I wanted to build a bank of memories that would sustain us through the tough times. We started small; I took them to Butlins when they were five, six, and seven years old. Then we progressed to Euro Disney in Paris, France, when the boys were eight, nine, and ten years old. When they were eleven, we went to Disney World in Florida. David loves the whole holiday experience; finding out where we are going, how we will get there, pre-holiday shopping, packing, the trip—the whole thing. So, in preparation for our Disney World trip, I told him that we were going on a big aeroplane, and we'd be on it for a long time. I explained Disney World was like Disneyland Paris but much bigger. He was excited—a good excited. The holiday was a huge success; David absolutely loved being on the plane. He behaved like an angel. We had little routines built into the holiday: We went to the same breakfast place every day (David's choice—Sizzler), then to one of the theme parks. After lunch, we'd go shopping at one of the outlet stores, then back to the hotel. We relaxed, used the hotel pool, and just had a nice time. Looking back, I think that was our best family holiday ever—we were so relaxed and happy. But the following year was our worst ever holiday experience.

The Florida holiday lulled me into a false sense of security, so I ignored that old saying, "If it aint broke, don't fix it." I decided to go somewhere different and chose Kos in Greece as our destination. As usual, a couple of months before the trip, I told David (Jonathan had known for some time) where and when we were going. He asked, "Disney?"

"No, David, not this time. Greece. It's going to be really good," I responded.

"David Disney," he insisted.

After a few days, he seemed to understand we weren't going on a Disney holiday, and we continued preparing as usual. I informed his school, and they wrote a Social Story to help him get ready. The day of the flight arrived, and we got a taxi to the airport. I'd bought a package holiday, with flights, hotels (half board—breakfast and dinner), and a couple of tours included. We boarded the aeroplane as usual—David's a pro at travelling, and I've never had any issues with air flights. However, for the first time, the twins' ears were hurting from the air pressure during the flight. I tried giving them boiled sweets and chewing gum to help reduce the pressure, but nothing worked. David was really good, and apart from moaning and covering his ears, he stayed fairly calm during the (thankfully) short flight. We disembarked from the plane and got a coach to the hotel. Everything seemed fine as we settled into our room and unpacked.

We went down for breakfast, and noticed the hotel had a pool. Perfect. Since the first scheduled tour wasn't until the next day, we decided to explore. There was a local water theme park about fifteen minutes from the hotel, so we decided to go there. We had a great time going on the different rides, getting wet. I allowed Jonathan to wander off on his own but agreed on a time and place to regroup. David was fairly happy but still had one thing on his mind.

"Disneyland Paris tomorrow?" He looked me directly in the face.

"No, David, this is Greece. It's a different place" I lowered my voice and tapped his arm.

"Aeroplane tomorrow, Disneyland," he insisted.

"No, Mummy hasn't got enough money for another ticket. Next year," I tried to reassure him. David knew I didn't make empty promises. I couldn't afford to—there'd be hell to pay afterwards, and it wasn't worth it.

"Disney tomorrow," he persisted, getting louder with each statement.

"David, we'll talk about it later."

He didn't forget and bought it up at every possible opportunity. After the second day, he realised that Disneyland wasn't happening, and boy, he made his displeasure known! Every night, all night, he would scream and hit himself. Nothing I did would console him. I had spoken to a chemist before the holiday and bought some over-the-counter sleeping tablets before the holiday as David has sleep issues, but they didn't make any difference; he was up for most of the night, suffering from meltdowns. I was at my wit's end, completely overwhelmed with feelings of immense guilt and frustration. The poor woman next door was very understanding—more than I felt that I deserved, but also frustrated. All she wanted was a holiday with her children, and they couldn't sleep because of David. She didn't say, but I'm convinced she thought to herself, "Why on earth would you take him on holiday?"

Over the years, I've often thought about her—she was a fellow Brit—and wish there was a way I could make it up to her.

I think both David and Jonathan would agree that was the worst holiday we've ever taken. At one point, David hit me for the first (and last) time. I'm ashamed to say I lost it. I screamed in his face, "Don't you ever touch me again. Don't try it. Just don't do it."

He backed off and quieted down for a bit, but Jonathan was in a constant state of hypervigilance in the aftermath of that incident. When we got home, he was afraid to leave David and I alone together. He was scared David would do something to me, or I would do something to David. It was a difficult time for us all.

After that holiday, we didn't go away as a family for six years. The next summer, David asked, "Holiday? Disney?"

"No! David doesn't behave on holidays, so no more holidays," I replied firmly.

He gave me his dazzling smile. "David sorry," signing sorry at the same time.

"No, it's too late. No more holiday."

His face dropped. "Next year?"

"No! It's too late."

"We'll see?" That was his way of saying "maybe."

"No!"

After three years of similar conversations, he changed tack. "Holiday, Spain? Greece?"

"No!"

In 2010, when David was 20 years old, I decided to be brave and try again. At this point, we hadn't been on a family holiday for 6 years I booked a self-catering holiday to Spain and warned David if there were any issues, they would be no more holidays ever! He was so happy and excited, he was in a good mood for the whole week, and I haven't had any issues since. But I learned not to be complacent where David was concerned.

Heath/Mental Health:

I'm blessed that even though I'm not fit, my physical health is generally good. However, during the teenage years, I felt like I was in a state of perpetual exhaustion. I was continually running on empty, working the night shift, and attending numerous meetings about David as all the professionals involved in David's life were becoming concerned about the escalation of his behaviour. I was permanently stressed. Looking back now, I was probably on the brink of depression. At the time, my whole focus was David and trying to manage the new challenges. I barely had the energy to see to Jonathan's well-being, which left even less time to consider my own needs.

I suffered from tension headaches regularly but started to get recurring headaches where it felt like a metal vice was crushing my head. My vision would become blurry, and I constantly felt dizzy. I went to see my doctor, convinced I had a tumour growing in my head. After an MRI scan, the results showed I was suffering from migraines.

Jonathan also suffered from headaches starting around age sixteen. At first, I thought, *he's too young to have headaches.* When they persisted, I sent him to see the doctor. It turned out he also had tension headaches and would eventually start developing migraines too. Just one more thing to add to the list of things I felt guilty about.

David and Jonathan both grew very quickly during their teenage years. They are both six-footers and quite strong. Between the ages of thirteen and fifteen, David's self-injurious behaviour intensified. He had stopped punching his face but would still slap himself with both hands with considerable force. It was extremely upsetting to watch, especially as if he hit a grown man with that much force, they'd be out cold. (Up to this point, David hadn't hit another person, apart from the incident with me in Greece.)

After some time with the slapping behaviour, I noticed something wrong with David's right eye. I'd initially thought it was hay fever, as the three of us suffer from this every spring and summer. But autumn came, and Jonathan and I no longer had red, swollen, puffy eyes; but David's right eye was constantly red and almost closing. Our GP referred us to Moorfield Eye Hospital, where they informed me that David had a detached retina; they also advised they wouldn't recommend the operation to re-attach it. Too much time had passed since the original injury, and the perceived benefits of the operation would not be worth undergoing such a significant, invasive procedure. After numerous tests, they determined David had 6/36 vision in his right eye. Today, David is blind in his right eye. I was heartbroken when I realised that, and felt guilty that I hadn't been able to prevent this from happening. I hadn't followed up on his eye problems in good time. I also believe that David's subsequent epilepsy diagnosis was a direct result of his self-injurious behaviour.

When David got upset, which was happened with more frequency in his teenage years, he would start lashing out and hitting anyone who got in his way. I started getting calls and complaints from the school, and David was eventually referred to the Child and Adolescent Mental Health Service (CAMHS) for support. We went for a few sessions, but I felt they just wanted to medicate him. When he was younger, I was strongly encouraged to put David on a course of Ritalin. I asked around and researched the drug but ultimately decided against it— I felt it would be much better to get rid of David's abundance of energy through physical activity. But at CAMHS, rightly or wrongly, I felt they had an agenda. They were asking me leading questions, and no matter how I tried to say David wasn't displaying some of the behaviours they were suggesting, they were going back over issues I didn't feel were relevant. I wasn't in denial—David was finding it difficult to control his emotions, was very unhappy, and his behaviour was escalating. I felt they were trying to fob me off and prescribe him medication to manage, not help, him. They recommended Risperidone, which, at that time, had only recently started to be prescribed for autistic children. According to my research at the time, it was an antipsychotic drug commonly used to treat Schizophrenia, and the side effects included increased appetite, rapid weight gain, and drowsiness. I was adamant about not letting anyone dope my child, and they didn't push any further.

Shortly after my sessions with CAMHS, a meeting was scheduled at the school with his social worker, educational psychologist, the head teacher, and his class teacher. I approached the school with a lot of apprehension, thinking I might be walking into an ambush, and they were going to tell me that they couldn't handle David's behaviour and would have to exclude him permanently. I was half right; it was an intervention of sorts. David was struggling, and the school didn't feel they had the tools to support him. They suggested I consider sending him to a residential school for autistic children in Broadstairs, Kent. They knew how protective I was of David and how resistant I had been to the idea of a boarding school in the past. They assured me the final decision was mine and told me that some staff from the residential school had already visited and observed David a few times. They felt David was a good fit and suggested Jonathan and I visit the school.

So, I did what they asked; I spoke to Jonathan, and we visited the school. Jonathan was surprised to see other children who appeared and behaved like David. Most of the autistic children we had met before the visit were verbal and articulate. We hadn't ever met children who presented like David. I subsequently visited the school with David and asked him if he liked it. I explained he would be sleeping there and would come home at weekends. We visited the accommodation area, looked at the bedrooms and living area, and toured the school. We met the teachers and observed a couple of classes before we went home.

I was torn; David was fifteen at the time, and we were all struggling. I confided in some of my friends at church and asked them to pray for me. I wasn't expecting the responses I got. They were roughly in three camps:

- "It's about time. You need to stop being a martyr and start thinking about yourself. You absolutely need to accept this offer. It's a no-brainer!"

- "You don't need to pray about it. You can't send David away. God knows what will happen to him—you hear all these stories about child abuse. We'll work something out; we'll support you better. Just don't send him away from under your protection."

- "I know this is hard for you, but I'm here for you. I'll pray for you. I know you'll make the right decision."

Unfortunately, the people who were against it kept going on and on about it, especially when I told them I'd decided to go for it. I felt tremendous pressure to change my mind and felt misunderstood. People were second-guessing the motives for my decisions. Some people thought I'd had enough and elected to "dump" David in a boarding school for an easier life. Others believed I thought my only way to snag a man was to get David out of the way. Nothing was further from the truth, and I felt unable to defend myself. In the end, I was so frustrated by everyone trying to tell me what to do, I lost it and snapped at one of my friends. I told her that I knew she was coming from a place of love, but I felt she was trying to control me. At forty years of age, I was quite capable of making decisions for my son! We did make up eventually, as this was completely out of character for me.

Once I told the school I was happy for David to move schools, the process to transfer him went quickly. The approval came during the summer term, so David started at his new school in the autumn. We drove up to the school with David and stayed all morning. David was in good spirits and didn't seem upset when we left. That week, I wasn't myself. I was distracted at work, couldn't sleep, couldn't eat. I asked myself if I'd done the right thing. I wondered if he was ok, if he was happy, how he was coping. The week dragged on; it felt like the longest week of my life.

Saturday came, and I perked up. I cooked David's favourite meal—jollof rice with fried plantain and chicken—and drove the two hours to Broadstairs with Jonathan. I was so happy to see David, but he seemed to be quite nonchalant when he saw me—the food got a bigger reaction than I did. I felt like saying "What about me? Am I chopped liver?"

The staff spoke to me and explained that there had been a few teething problems, but nothing they hadn't expected. David seemed to be adapting to his new routine and enjoying it. I think because he was used to being away from home for respite care, the adjustment to staying somewhere else wasn't as big a deal as I had expected it to be. In fact, I was the one who was struggling to adapt; David was fine.

I was relieved that David was happy, and Jonathan could see I wasn't just dumping his brother in a boarding school for my own motives—I made sure I included Jonathan in all the decisions that involved David. I wanted to ensure he understood everything that happened to his brother.

For the next four years, our new routine was this: David came home after three weeks for the weekend (Friday afternoon until – Monday morning). He stayed at school for three weeks, then came home for the half-term week. He also came home for the holidays. My brother Kunle was a lifesaver! He helped with the pick-ups and drop-offs when David came home. A coach would drop David off in Battersea Park at around 1 p.m. on the Fridays he came home, and he had to be there by 1 p.m. on the Mondays he went back for the return trip. Prior to his time at boarding school, I left the post office and started studying to become a British Sign Language interpreter.

The timing was just right—Jonathan had his GCSE final exams, and I was nearing the end of my degree. We could study without being distracted and disturbed. When I completed my degree, I started working as a Communication Support Worker, supporting Deaf students in college. I couldn't manage the drop-offs and pick-ups because of my schedule; however, this meant I had half terms and school holidays off, so I could be with David. I travelled to Broadstairs fairly frequently for annual reviews and school shows. David had settled into his new school and was happy; he wrote letters home weekly, telling us how he was getting on. The staff noted in his file that we were Christians and regular churchgoers. In fact, David loves going to church, especially the song service, and looks forward to going every Sunday, so it has always been an important part of his routine. There were a fair number of Christian staff members, and they organised makeshift services on a Sunday for a few of the students—mainly singing church songs and having a short prayer. This really reassured me I'd made the right decision.

With David at school, I had the much-needed one-on-one time with Jonathan, who I felt I had neglected in favour of his brother all this time. But he was going through his rebellious stage and didn't really want to spend time with me. I was hurt, but I understood—he'd had to be self-reliant all those years, and though I'd tried my best, I hadn't been there for him the way he'd needed. And when he was dipping his feet into adulthood and didn't need me breathing down his neck, there I was. However, it was a time I was grateful to have, to be able to have uninterrupted quality time with Jonathan.

David always seemed to be jealous when I spent time with Jonathan and not him; he would interrupt and start making noise (he still does).

Jonathan wasn't a bad kid. We're similar temperament-wise, so we managed to muddle through this period, stealing moments together when he'd allow it. Finally, one day when he was about twenty years old, I realised we were having proper conversations again. Yes! Finally, I had my son back!

Did You Know?

Tantrums and Meltdowns

Challenging behaviour is a term that parents of autistic children are familiar with. The stares, comments, judgment, and negative attitudes from people who don't know their child (and sometimes from those who do know their child) are part of their everyday lives. The big question is, why do autistic children (and adults) behave the way they do?

Most people who witness a child screaming, kicking, or generally acting out would assume the child is having a tantrum and is spoilt or badly behaved. However, if the child is autistic, it's more likely they're having a meltdown. You might think it's the same thing, but it's not.

Tantrum:

This is when a child is trying to get what they want by kicking, screaming, biting, throwing things, and other violent behaviour. They are usually frustrated because they cannot get what they want or do what they want to do. They typically know what they are doing and can control or stop themselves. Tantrums can generally be quelled by giving the child what they want, comforting the child, or ignoring them, Or by making the child choose between changing to correct behaviour or a consequence for choosing bad behaviour (such as losing a favourite toy, not being able to do an activity, or even a punishment

Meltdown:

This can look like a tantrum but is caused by overstimulation or sensory overload. Meltdowns happen in autistic children, teens, and adults. They can happen with or without an audience and tend to last longer than tantrums. It occurs when they are overwhelmed by too much sensory, emotional, or information input or too much unpredictability. They can't control their meltdowns, and you can't stop them; you need to let the meltdowns run their course. However if you can remove either some of the stimulation or remove them from the situation where they are being overstimulated, it can sometimes help them to calm quicker.

You can make sure they are safe and don't hurt themselves, develop a routine to help them calm down once the meltdown is over, and stay calm yourself.

Helpful Hints

Keeping Your Child Safe

It is hard to deal with and support teenagers and young adults through puberty and discovering their sexuality at the best of times. Throw autism into the mix, and it becomes even more daunting. Puberty can be a confusing time for young autistic people, and as parents and carers, sometimes we struggle to support them effectively; especially when we do not know how to deal with some of the behaviours they display.

Many autistic individuals engage in inappropriate sexual behaviour because of a lack of social awareness. Such behaviours include uninhibited masturbating, unwanted touching of others, use of sexualised language, and risky online behaviour (sexting, accessing illegal pornography, illicit chat rooms, etc). It's important that we have the necessary tools to teach and support our youngsters and start early.

- Use social stories and role play to explain what happens during puberty,[17] demonstrate what appropriate behaviour looks like, and teach them to ask for support when they are upset or uncomfortable.[18]

- Protect your child from their online activity ensuring the devices they use are secure; making sure that they have up to date antivirus, anti-spyware and anti-spam/phishing software installed, and that privacy settings are enabled.

- Support your child to create a secure password, and screen name.

- Demonstrate internet safety, using their preferred communication style, Social Stories, role play, visual methods, and tailored training material.

- Teach the importance of not posting anything online when they are upset; that it's not safe to share personal information online; what trolling is, and techniques to try and avoid it.

- Discuss topics such as sexting, appropriate online behaviour, and why it's not safe to physically contact people they may meet online. These subjects need to be taught in a way that they can understand. But one of the most important safeguards, is that they have someone that they trust to talk to when they are unsure what to do, upset or feeling pressured.

- Sexting and online grooming are big concerns for people supporting autistic and vulnerable people; so, it is necessary to teach them about the dangers of these actions in a way that they will understand.

- Research Autism has a self-help guide about sex education that can help you start the conversation around sex education and sexual health with your children: https://researchautism.org/sex-ed-guide/

CHAPTER 8

School's Out Forever – What's Next?

Transition to adulthood

David's four years at Bradstow School passed swiftly. Before I knew it, he was in his final year, and I had to face the fact that he would be home, and I didn't know where to go or what to do next. I investigated what he could do next, but I couldn't find any services for young autistic adults. There was a plethora of services for children, a few for older people, but provision for young adults was few and far between.

Thomas May, a transitional social worker with the learning disability team, was assigned to be David's social worker during his transition from children's services to adult service. He was great! Together, we explored the placements and resources available for young autistic adults. He gave me a prospectus of all the colleges that catered for adults with learning disabilities or autism in the UK. Tom made me realise that David probably wouldn't thrive if he stayed home with me, but also respected I wanted David close to home. I wanted to see David whenever I felt like and not be constrained by distance. We focussed our search in London and the South East of the United Kingdom: the Home Counties (Kent, Surrey, Sussex, Berkshire, and Buckinghamshire).

Thomas was amazing and extremely thorough. He did a ton of research and shortlisted the homes he felt were a good match for David. He created a schedule, and we visited six homes, spoke to the staff, and observed the residents. We were also allowed to look at a couple of the rooms in each home (with the resident's permission). They were a mixed bag; the staff all appeared friendly and nice, and the homes were alright, but nothing jumped out at me to say it could be David's new home. But the last one we visited was different. The company described itself as catering to young adults with autism, learning disabilities, and complex needs. The idea was they would take placements for people aged 19–25 years old, and the homes would become their permanent homes—where they would grow old together. The rooms were modern, spacious, bright, and airy. The residents were of mixed ability and had varying levels of needs, and I had a good feeling about it. The home was about an hour and a half away from my house, and I felt confident that David would fit in and settle down well.

On the drive home, I shared my feelings with Thomas; he told me that home had no vacancies, but they had several others in Surrey and Middlesex. He started the ball rolling and set up meetings with the organisation—London Care Partnership (LCP). Things seemed to be moving smoothly and swiftly. Then everything screeched to a halt!

Thomas told me he was leaving Wandsworth Council (my local authority area). Reading between the lines, I could tell he was overworked and burnt out; I was sad to see him go but knew he was doing the best thing for his health and sanity. Before Thomas left, he drew up comprehensive handover notes for his successor and wrote me a letter outlining what had been done and agreed to so far and what the next steps were. But after he left, there was a period where nothing seemed to happen.

I waited about a month to hear who was taking over David's case. Then, I called the Learning Disability Transitions team to try and get some answers. The social worker on duty took my call, wrote down my details, and promised someone would contact me. A week later, I hadn't heard anything, so I called back to chase up on the progress of my enquiry. A different duty social worker answered the phone. She was extremely apologetic and promised me she would look into it herself and get back to me within a week. She didn't. For the next two months, I called weekly but got nowhere. I found out they recruited two locum (temporary) social workers to replace Thomas. I was given the name of someone who had been allocated David's case but was never able to get hold of her. Spring was approaching, David was leaving school in summer, and I didn't know what would happen. I was worried I would have to give up work and claim welfare benefits to care for David. I have always worked and was under a lot of stress at this point.

Eventually, I snapped. I couldn't take the uncertainty anymore. I wrote a letter to the head of the Learning Disability Team at Wandsworth Social Services, explaining my predicament, praising Tom to the heavens, explaining what he had left in place to do, and criticizing the team for continually fobbing me off and treating me as a nuisance. I also sent a copy of the letter to the Director of Social Services at Wandsworth Council.

Three days later, I received a call at work. It was the Head of the Learning Disability team. He apologised profusely for the long delay in picking up David's case and assured me nobody was fobbing me off. He gave me a name of a (different) social worker who would be taking on David's case and promised she would contact me within the week. Sure enough, the social worker called me two days later and made a date to visit me at home the following week.

The new social worker came to see me one evening after work. The meeting was interesting; she had a copy of my letter in a file and started by saying that she felt all children should be treated the same and receive the same quality of service provision, not just those whose parents shouted the loudest. I was seething but bit my tongue and kept my cool. I pointed out that I had been calling and asking for help for three months before I resorted to writing my letter. I explained how far we had progressed under Tom's care and that I had chosen a placement with London Care Partnership. She was reluctant to proceed with this—I didn't understand why, and she wouldn't tell me. She insisted we visit the last two homes on the original list, one in Kent and the other in Surrey, so I accompanied her to look at them. Even though I'd already made up my mind, the two homes didn't impress me. I told her I wanted to go ahead with London Care Partnership, and finally, she started moving forward with it.

I met the owner, Greg, with the social worker in attendance, and he gave me the full spiel about the organisation, how they worked, and what they could offer. Several meetings were held at the school, my home, and the Town Hall (for Social Services) to discuss the possibility of David being placed there. Staff from LCP went to Bradstow School to observe David and talk with his teachers.

Greg told me that LCP had purchased a former children's home and were converting it into a house for their new intake of residents. He proposed that David move into that home. He described the location—on the border of Richmond and Barnes, with a river flowing nearby and opposite a primary school. As he described the location, I had a vague nagging feeling of familiarity, but I couldn't place what it was. Finally, the day came to visit the place. They had started work to convert it into an eight-bed home and warned me it was still a building site. My mother was paying her annual summer visit from Nigeria at the time, so Jonathan, mum, and I set off to see the place where David would end up moving.

    I entered the postcode into my satnav and started driving. Twenty minutes into the journey, Jonathan said: "This is the way to uncle Kunle's house!" He was right, every turning took me closer to where my brother lived, and when we arrived at our destination, it was a three-minute walk to my brother's flat. I was amazed and took it as a sign that it was meant to be. Greg was waiting with a woman at the house. He introduced us to Gina, the new home manager, and talked us through their plans. They were aiming for the home to be open by the end of July. Mum felt there was no way it would be ready by then (her exact words were "No way! It's not possible!"), but Greg was confident it would. The plans were ambitious; eight bedrooms, each with ensuite bathrooms on the first floor, a sleep-in room for staff, a meeting room, and a sensory room. It would be softly furnished with coloured lights and soft music piping through the room. Downstairs was a large living room area, a smaller computer room, a chill-out room, a dining room separate from the kitchen, and the office. There was also a spacious garden, to which they added a man-size swing and a giant trampoline.

    The next time David came down for the weekend, I explained he would be finishing school soon, and after he'd come back home for a bit, he'd be moving into a new place near his uncle's house. We introduced him to Gina, and they started to develop a relationship and an understanding. The building works progressed rapidly and was completed on schedule. We (Mum, David, Jonathan, and I) went on a tour of the completed home, and Georgina encouraged David to pick out his room. He picked the biggest room, and his bathroom was double the size of our family bathroom! Oh, the perks of being the first resident!

Before I knew it, the end of the school year had arrived, and David was home. I couldn't believe that chapter in our lives was closed. For so long, this had been our norm, and David was about to step into the next phase of his life. David was looking forward to the move, while I had mixed feelings about it. On the one hand, David was taking a step towards independence and adulthood, no longer relying on just me to support him and advocate for him. On the other hand, even though he'd been at boarding school for four years and had regularly had respite stays away from home over the years, this time, he would be moving out for good. Yes, he would still come home regularly for visits, but technically he would no longer live with me.

The days before David moved in passed quickly. We visited the home at Arabella Drive more frequently, getting to know the staff and David's new keyworker. Gina worked with David to establish his likes, dislikes, hobbies, and interests to create a schedule for him before he moved in.

On the morning of the move, I was tearful. I cooked a full English breakfast—toast, sausages, bacon, fried eggs, baked beans, and hash browns (but no mushrooms or black pudding—double yuck!). After breakfast, we finished packing David's things and loaded the car, ready to set off to help him move in. To my surprise, David said, "No, Mummy. David big man. David, Jonathan. Arabella Drive."

He didn't want me to take him there! He wanted to go with his brother. While preparing him for the move, I had repeatedly told him he was a big man now and showed him other people who were his age that he knew who had moved out of their parents' home; he felt he didn't want his mum tagging along as he made his next step. I was sad but honoured his request. For the first time in his life, I wasn't involved in a major milestone. I was proud of him—it was the first time I acknowledged that David was an adult and was capable of making his own decisions.

So, Jonathan drove his brother to his new home and helped him unpack and settle in. He stayed with him for a few hours and came home to tell me that everything was ok, and David was fine. I tried not to be *that* mum, the helicopter mum, but I couldn't help myself. I called every day to check on him but forced myself not to go and see him for a week. As usual, David was fine while I was a total wreck! My brother checked in with him regularly and reported back to me that David was fine. On one occasion when he turned up, David said, "Hello Uncle Kunle. Bye," and went back to what he was doing—baking shortbread! (How rude!) I was relieved to know he was comfortable and secure where he was.

As always, I felt guilty—I was his mother, so I should be able to take care of him. But I grew to see that David had the best of both worlds. He lived in a home where people could cater to his needs and do the things he loved with him, and he came home every weekend and holiday to spend time with his brother and me. David would frequently go on walks and bike rides, and to see the deer in the nearby Richmond Park. They set up a routine, which included swimming, bowling, and visits to the adventure playground. But David wanted to go to college—actually, he wanted to go to university. I think his reasoning was mum went to university, Jonathan's going to university, so why not him?

He had left school with no formal qualifications. He had the ASDAN Bronze award; ASDAN is an awarding body that provides curriculum to prepare students for employment and independence; as part of their offer, they have courses for students with special education needs. I persuaded David that he needed to go to college, not university, and he agreed to go.

We registered him with a local college, South Thames College in Wandsworth, where he did a life skills course for students with learning disabilities. He loved attending the college, especially as our family had links to the college—his aunt and one of his uncles studied there, his brother did a course there, and I worked there occasionally. It was nice that David could be part of that family tradition. David never attended a mainstream school, so he liked being a part of a "normal" college and not being segregated. He knew he was different but always wanted to try and fit in.

At that time, I worked in an agency based in a local school for Deaf children, which sent me out to local colleges to support Deaf students. I remember talking to a colleague, and somehow during the conversation, I started to talk about David. As I described him and explained he went to South Thames College, she exclaimed, "I know him! I see him all the time!" and started telling me what she'd seen him do.

Another time, I had a meeting with a deaf member of the college staff but didn't have my college ID pass on me, so I had to go through reception. As I signed in, the receptionist read my name and interjected, "We have a young man with the same name who comes here."

"I know. He's my son." I smiled as I responded.

"Really? Wow! He's such a handsome young man. What's wrong with him?"

"He's autistic." I didn't have the time or inclination to start a conversation about the fact that I felt there was nothing wrong with him.

"Oh, that's a shame. How come?" She continued, unaware of how she came across.

"Nobody knows. He has a twin who isn't autistic. It's just one of those things." I hoped that she would leave it there. I wasn't ready to get into it with her.

Her face dropped. "Oh no! That's so sad." I couldn't understand why people thought this way.

I started walking away. "I really must be going now; I'm going to be late for my meeting."

"Oh! Ok, you have a nice day. Bye."

I really hated those kinds of conversations. I tried not to take it personally; I knew people meant well, but it really irks me that people see David as defective, not as a unique individual in his own right.

David stayed at South Thames College for two years. On the day of his "graduation," I was sad as neither Jonathan nor I was free to attend—the school gave us notice only two days before the event. But my parents were visiting from Nigeria at the time and were happy to go see him graduate—it was the first time in about seventeen years David had seen his granddad. My father died later that year, so I was glad that they got a chance to see each other before he passed.

At the end of the two years, we looked for another course for David to enrol in, but unfortunately, they didn't have any other courses appropriate for him. David was keen to continue at South Thames College; I think it helped him feel like everyone else, doing the things that "normal" young people did, but unfortunately, it wasn't to be. Eventually, we found some courses to enrol him in at Richmond Adult Education College: understanding money, basic cooking, basic IT, and Zumba. David liked his new college well enough, but he preferred his old one, and every time we passed it (it was between home and Arabella Drive), he would tell me "David, South Thames College." He did this for years, and even now, eight years after he left, he still mentions it occasionally.

All in all, David attended college for about five years; he exhausted everything they had locally, and he was too bright to repeat the same thing over and over again. He decided he wanted to work—his mum went to work, and his brother went to work, so why not him? Why not indeed! Unfortunately, finding David a job was easier said than done.

David is a nice, healthy, strong young man, and he's a good gardener, so we thought we'd be able to find him a job or volunteer role in a gardening setting. We did some research and found an organisation which we thought would be a perfect match. I'd heard about this organisation from my work as a Communication Support Worker, and they were located near my home. But when we looked into it in more detail, we realised David would have to pay to attend. I was quite indignant at what I felt was an attempt to get cheap (or free) labour by taking advantage of a vulnerable group. Looking back now, I feel I may have been harsh in my judgment, but at the time, it was yet another obstacle in David's quest to become a productive member of the community.

David always helped with the gardening at Arabella Drive. At home it was another story. I couldn't get David to work in the garden, no matter what I tried. Bribes, threats, pleading, feigned anger—nothing worked. He would become extremely vocal and loud, so I'd just give up. I couldn't take the noise. Even if everyone was working in the garden, he wouldn't budge. So, when they sang his praises for his garden work at school and Arabella Drive, I just shook my head. It was as if they were talking about a different person. I think David feels he doesn't have anything to prove to me, and that's why he refuses to do it. He's a people pleaser, but I believe he's comfortable enough at home to say "no" to me. And as much as I wish I could benefit from his gardening skills, I'm happy that he knows he can say no to things he doesn't want. It's taken him a long time to get there.

Gina, the manager at Arabella Drive, bought David his own gardening tools—gloves, a broom, and a shovel—and they paid him £10 a week to help tidy the garden every morning. He seemed happy with the arrangement and used his money to treat himself to hot chocolate and biscuits at Starbucks every week.

About two years ago, we found an organisation that had a project working with young adults with learning disabilities restoring stately homes and their gardens. David liked the idea of going to work in a proper garden, but unfortunately, the project dates were every Thursday. He went to the adventure playground every Thursday and really enjoyed the activities he did there and didn't want to give up that day. But he really wanted to work too. So, I suggested a compromise—alternate weeks at both activities. David was quite happy with this arrangement; he felt he had a purpose, something people depended on him to do, so he started a new routine—gardening every other Thursday. He had a fixed routine, doing things he enjoyed doing with people who understood him. He seemed settled, and life was good.

Did You Know?

Transitioning Is Difficult

As difficult as it is, the process of getting your child into and through secondary school is actually the easy bit. The challenges autistic children face during the transition to adult services are numerous and sometimes it feels that the services for autistic people stop when they become adults. Some of the barriers faced include:

- Difficulties maintaining consistent staffing of professionals involved over the transition period

- A lack of communication between professionals in different services and the parents about what is being planned

- Not having enough well-resourced services available for autistic adults

- The need to pay for services that were provided free when the autistic person was a child

- Carers not always included in consultations about their family member who is now an adult

- Many autistic people feel a listlessness and loss of structure when they leave school, as the school setting is very structured and day-to-day scheduling is uniform. The sudden lack of this can leave a young autistic person wondering, "What am I supposed to be doing? Why am I not following my schedule?"

- Difficulties coping with change

- The limited provision of further education options, especially for those who display challenging behaviour.
- When transition plans fail, autistic people can end up stuck in poor-quality services that fail to meet their needs

Helpful Hints

How to Ensure Successful Transition Planning

Get a head start and begin planning early. Transition planning usually starts in Year 10 in the UK, the year before children's final year in school. Your best bet is to start towards the end of year 9 and research, research, research, and then research some more!

Find out what is available, and don't limit your search to your local area. Resources and services for autistic adults are not as abundant as they are for children, so it's important that you don't limit your options.

Remember to keep your child involved in your plans; person-centred planning is key to ensuring that your child's wishes, and feelings are considered when you are planning their future.

Consider all the options available: further education and training, employment support, volunteering options, residential or supported living, day services, befriending or mentoring. You can narrow down your options later.

How to Advocate for Your Child and Ensure You Get the Services They Need:

Understand the procedures around annual review meetings and make sure they are followed.

You know your child best. Understand and share the strategies and techniques that work with your child so people who may work with them in the future know how to engage with them.

Share information about your child's sensory needs so their new education or residential setting can be set up in a way that meets their needs.

Work together with your child to create their personal communication passport. This will give people information about their communication preferences. You can find templates for this online to download or purchase.

Talk to organisations like Citizen's Advice, the National Autistic Society and Contact-A-Family for information and advice on services available for autistic adults. Find out where you can get advocacy services—someone that can speak up and advocate for the rights and desires of your child.

CHAPTER 9

The Empty Nest

Creating a New Normal after Your Children Move Out

After David had settled into his new routine, Jonathan and I settled into our own new normal. Jonathan started university a couple of months after David moved out, and I had just become self-employed. The recession of 2008 hit charities and local authorities very hard, and both my places of work had cut my hours. I couldn't afford to live on my earnings, and my bank account was constantly in the red. I wasn't business-minded and the thought of being self-employed terrified me, but I had no choice. I spoke to some of my friends in the same profession and took the plunge—and haven't looked back since. Obviously, there have been ups and downs; there were five months when I didn't have an income, had exhausted all my savings, and was really worried about losing my home. And there have been times when I've had a lot of work coming in, am getting paid on time, and financially buoyant. During those times, I always worry—when is it going to happen? When is my situation going to take a turn for the worse? But all in all, it's been going well.

We had established a routine; David came home every weekend, all the bank holidays, a couple of weeks in August, and a week over Christmas. And for the first time in their lives, the twins no longer celebrated their birthdays together unless it fell on a Friday, Saturday, or Sunday. This was huge and took some adjusting, but if David gets to speak to his brother on their birthday, he's fine; and Jonathan usually makes time to do something with him, just the two of them after the day. It's funny, David loves celebrating his birthday, and Jonathan isn't too keen, but does it because of his twin.

Having settled into our new ways of living, Jonathan started dating. The church we'd been attending for over fifteen years at the time had strong beliefs on dating and marriage. They considered dating to be a very serious decision. Specifically, if you chose to date someone, it meant you see yourself potentially marrying that person, and "courting" shouldn't last more than a year. The reasoning behind this is a year is enough time to see if you're compatible and dating for more than a year would make it difficult to stay celibate in the relationship. This meant many couples married young. Jonathan and Rianna were twenty-one and eighteen when they started dating; I had mixed feelings about their relationship. Rianna is a lovely young lady, beautiful on the inside and outside, but I was concerned that they were too young. Both had lived relatively sheltered lives, and I was worried they weren't yet ready for a real relationship. Jonathan had just recommitted himself to his faith about a year before he embarked on his relationship with Rianna. He'd drifted away from the church when he was about fifteen and only attended because I made him go. At the time, I could see his heart wasn't in it, and under other circumstances, I would say it's counterproductive to force a young person to do something they didn't want to do, but I felt I had to. At the time, young black boys in the UK, but particularly in London, were being killed at an unbelievable rate. Jonathan knew a few of the boys that had been murdered. The thought of losing him petrified me, and being in church helped. The practice of stop and search by the police was so commonplace, after the first few times he was stopped (at age ten or eleven), he didn't bother telling me. He said he stopped running to catch buses, as nine times out of ten, he'd be stopped by the police and told he fit the description of someone they were after—even when he was smartly dressed.

Our church had many activities, especially for young people. Jonathan was involved in the youth drama group, and it kept him very busy. Between work, studies, and church, he had no time to get into trouble. The period between fifteen and nineteen was very stressful. It was touch and go as to which path he'd take, and it petrified me that I might lose him to crime, and he'd become another statistic—yet another young black boy from a single-parent family who was engaged in criminal activity. So, being so fully engaged in church and church activities answered my prayers. At the same time, the amount of time and effort he was putting into the drama group, especially when it was coming up to the time a play was about to be performed, concerned me greatly. He was getting home around midnight, so I was still a bundle of nerves, constantly on the phone to the leader of the group, wanting to know what time they were finishing and what time Jonathan would be home. I know they saw me as a nuisance, an overprotective mother who was mollycoddling her son, but I didn't care. I watched the news; I saw the statistics; I knew how society judged the mothers of the boys, and he was my son! I was also worried about his studies. He was approaching his final year in university, and I didn't think he gave it as much attention as he needed. As it turned out, he realised he was doing too much and took an extra year to finish.

After dating for a year, Jonathan and Rianna got engaged. David was delighted by the news, telling everyone "David, Jonathan, Rianna wedding." I had to sit him down to explain, "No, David. Jonathan and Riana are getting married. Yes, David and Mummy will be there, but after the wedding, Jonathan and Rianna are going to their own home."

Jonathan proposed on Rianna's twentieth birthday, and the wedding was on the June 1st of the following year. Everyone had an opinion about how the wedding should be. I had to remind my extended family that I was the mother of the groom and not the bride's mother, the couple was British born and bred, and Rianna wasn't from a Nigerian background. I offended some family and friends of the family by not extending invitations (we were expected to throw a big society wedding). My response? It's not my wedding, and I don't want mother-in-law/daughter-in-law problems before they're even married. Jonathan and Rianna had no idea about the arguments I had with my very traditional mum, who wanted things done 100% according to our culture.

I was keen that Jonathan felt comfortable inviting his father and family from his father's side of the family without worrying about upsetting me—not everyone in my family felt the same. His dad couldn't make it, but his grandfather and two of his uncles came. The wedding day came and went; David had a wonderful time. The church service, the reception, food, drink speeches—he absolutely loved it. The wedding photos show David beaming like the proverbial Cheshire cat. I was a bundle of emotions. I was happy for Jonathan and Rianna; I felt that I must have done something right for him to reach that major milestone in his life. But it felt like the end of an era—my last born was leaving home. I always told my friends that they should allow their sons to leave them and cleave to their wives as the Bible taught. But the reality of that saying began to hit home, "A son is a son till he takes a wife, a daughter is a daughter for life."

I felt bereft after I got home—both boys had left home. But in the early hours of the next morning, Jonathan called me. "Mum, can you do me a favour?"

"Of course! What do you need?" I was puzzled but not alarmed. He sounded okay, so I wondered what was going on.

"I left my passport in my room. Could you bring it for me in the morning, please? My flight leaves at 11:00. My hotel is near the airport, so I can meet you at the North Terminal."

I was secretly thrilled. I thought to myself, *"He still needs me. I haven't been completely relegated"*.

I found his passport and took a train to Gatwick Airport early the next morning—a thirty-five-minute journey. Jonathan came out to meet me, we had a quick chat, and he hugged me before I left (Jonathan is not big on hugging, so this was huge for me).

I spent the next couple of weeks sorting out post-wedding logistics, calling and thanking people for their support, returning their suits and rented items, and generally recovering from the day. I had missed a couple of church services—my attendance had dropped to only Sunday morning in the prior year. In the past, I attended all the services, including the Wednesday mid-week service, Friday home bible study, and Sunday evening service. I found it increasingly difficult to keep up with my busy schedule after I hit my forties. By the time Jonathan and Rianna got married, I was forty-seven, and my body had started to slow down.

One of my younger church friends, Patricia, called me to see how I was getting on.

"How are you, Aunty Tayo? The wedding was lovely. You've done well with the boys. You must be so proud of Jonathan."

We made some conversation, and she ended by saying, "See you in church."

"No, you won't. I'm not coming back to church," I responded. Straight away, I thought, *Wow! Where did that come from*? I had no idea that was going to come out of my mouth, and although subconsciously, I'd been thinking of leaving the church, I hadn't decided yet. Well, I didn't realise I had.

"But why, Aunty Tayo? Now isn't the time! What about Jonathan?"

"What about Jonathan?" I responded. " He's married now. You know, leave and cleave!"

Patricia tried to dissuade me from my decision, but having articulated it, I was adamant—that was what I was going to do. After all, it was now or never. I could no longer use the boys as a reason for staying in church; I had to make my decisions for myself.

Over the next few weeks, I received numerous phone calls from friends and leaders in the church questioning my decision and trying to persuade and coerce me into changing my mind. I felt tremendous pressure to give in; my mum hadn't yet returned to Nigeria and thought I should just give in for an easy life, but I stood strong. I hadn't been happy in the church for a while. I was pleased with their focus on youth, nurturing the youngsters, and ensuring their lives stayed on track. But I felt this was at the expense of the older mature members. I also supported their stance on marriage, but I felt I wasn't respected or valued, especially by the younger married couples because I was a single mother. The fact that the church was very patriarchal just added to my discomfort, and I felt my time there had come to a natural end after nineteen years.

Poor Jonathan! He was completely unaware of this and was completely unprepared for his first day back at church after his honeymoon! He was bombarded with questions and was so confused. What was everyone talking about?

"Is it true your mum has left the church?"

"Why did your mum leave?"

"You need to talk to your mum and get her to change her mind!" (This was from one of my good friends.)

I finally got to speak to him and explained my reasons. He didn't fully understand at the time, but he respected my decision. He spoke to all the naysayers and told them I hadn't abandoned my faith but was just moving on.

Finally, the day I never thought would happen had arrived. I was home alone. My boys were all grown up and had moved out, and I didn't know what to do with myself. You think you know what empty nest syndrome is, but you don't really. Not until you become an empty nester yourself.

I felt so alone. I'm an introvert by nature, and I'm very happy in my own company, often the craving for alone time is like a physical ache. But nothing prepared me for the intense solitude of living alone. I missed my boys terribly. I missed the sounds of them moving around, David's noises, casual conversations with Jonathan, arguing over the TV, cooking meals for them. I missed being mum. David came home every weekend, but it wasn't the same without Jonathan; David missed his brother too. And because I'd left the church, I didn't get to see him on the weekends as much. My desire to have a good relationship with my daughter-in-law and not be the trope of the overbearing mother-in-law meant I backed off and did my best not to come into the middle of their relationship. Before they got married, I told Jonathan I'd only visit by invitation. As much as I wanted to be in their lives, I didn't want to become a nuisance and outstay my welcome.

I'd spent twenty-three years focusing on being a good mother to my twins; now, I was bereft. I threw myself into work and started visiting other churches. I eventually settled in my current church. I felt a sense of coming home the first time I walked into the building. I had been praying that I wanted to use my Sign Language skills to serve God in some way, and halfway through my first visit to the church, a deaf acquaintance bumped into me. Funnily enough, I'd recently seen her at a Deaf Christian meeting for the first time in a few years. She told me about how she'd been attending her church for years with no interpreter, but she hadn't given up on God answering her prayers and sending one to the church. I felt it was a sign that this was to be my new church home.

David adjusted quickly. After a few Sundays of asking, "Old church? New church? Jonathan, Rianna?" he settled in. I started interpreting the service into Sign Language, sitting next to Deborah, my Deaf friend. I also discovered the home life group nearest to me was the same one Deborah attended. It felt like everything was lining up seamlessly for me—this was where I was supposed to be. A few weeks after I started attending the church, Deborah invited Jackie, another Deaf friend, to church. That Sunday, Deborah wasn't in church. I recognised Jackie when she came in; she was my sister's friend. I went up to meet her, showed her where I was sitting (near the front), and started signing to her.

"No, no, no. This won't work. You have to move to the front; I'm going to get a crick in my neck here," Jackie signed.

My heart sank. That was the last thing I wanted, all eyes on me as I waved my hands about in the front of the church!

"I'm new here, I'm not sure about this. I don't even know who to ask," I responded half-heartedly.

But Jackie wasn't having it—there's a reason her sign name is "stubborn"! She waved to get the attention of an usher. When they came over, I explained our predicament. The usher got me a chair and placed it at the front of the auditorium, to the left of the stage. Jackie went and sat in a pew opposite me; that was the beginning of the Deaf Ministry in the church. I was mortified! My heart was pounding, and my mouth was dry. Anytime I looked around, it felt like everyone was staring at me, wondering who on earth I was and what in the world I was doing.

After the service ended, I approached the associate pastor, explained what had transpired (I didn't want him to think I'd taken it on myself to re-arrange how the service was conducted, and plonked myself at the front of the auditorium, stealing his thunder in the process). I introduced Jackie to him; he was very gracious and took it in his stride when Jackie proceeded to interrogate him about Sign Language access in the church and the need for church leaders to be Deaf Aware. Over the ensuing years, Pastor Collin turned out to be a champion for the Deaf members of the congregation, and a huge supporter of the growing Deaf Ministry.

Did You Know?

Autism and Adults

Often people with caring responsibilities tend not to think about looking after their own needs. However, if you don't look after your own health and wellbeing, you won't have the inner resources you need to do everything you need to do well for your autistic child or adult. If you are a carer for a child or adult in the United Kingdom, you are entitled to a Carer's assessment to determine the effects of your caring role on you and other areas of your life. You can get information about how to request a Carer's Assessment from your nearest Carer's centre, or from the Adult Social Care department from your local authority. Unfortunately, the Local Authority is only duty bound to provide an assessment, and often don't always provide the services or resources that have been identified are needed because of the assessment.

Age UK has a handy checklist for carers that helps to identify services and resources to ensure carers make the most of the help and assistance they can receive. It covers the direct support for the carer and their wellbeing, finances, work, and support for the person they care for. The checklist can be accessed here: https://www.ageuk.org.uk/globalassets/age-uk/documents/information-guides/age-uk-carers-checklist.pdf

If you haven't already done so, contact the National Autistic Society, the Carer's Centre and/or Citizen's Advice to see if they can support you to get the help you need and to find out if there are any benefits, resources or services that you are entitled to as a Carer.

CHAPTER 10

Why Is My Brother Like This?

A Sibling's Perspective, by Jonathan Ogundeji

My very earliest memories in life start at four years old. At this age, I remember being aware that I could talk, and my twin brother couldn't. At this point, nothing seemed unusual to me; I accepted everything I saw as the way things were. I remember the people at the church we attended at the time found it difficult to manage my brother, as he was very hyperactive and had a lot of energy to burn. One day, David was running up and down—as usual—and ran outside the church building into the street. By the time I got outside, I remember seeing him lying in the middle of the road in front of a car. I didn't process what had happened at the time or even realise the severity of the situation; in fact, the panic of everyone around and David being rushed to the hospital made the situation seem exciting—it was like something you would see on TV or a cool story for me to tell my friends later on.

Whilst I cannot remember every detail in the aftermath of that incident, I remember feeling a distinctive difference in how David was treated in that church compared to myself; at this point, my understanding was that he couldn't talk and liked to misbehave. In response to his behaviour, the ushers strapped his arms to a chair when he was sitting down. I didn't think there was anything wrong with this at the time, especially since I remember David always being happy during that time. I don't recall him seeming upset or angry; he was a very happy boy. Even in that chair, David didn't seem to have any complaints. It seemed so normal to me, I didn't even realise at the time why my mum was so upset at this, and why we left the church. But again, at this age, I didn't have a lot of questions; I just took things as they were and accepted that suddenly, we were moving to another church.

We moved churches when we were five years old, and at this age, I started to have a lot of questions; there were significantly more kids in that church than my old one, and I remember joining Sunday school. We had been to Sunday school before, but I started to notice a very clear difference between David and all the other kids, including myself. I went to Sunday school, and he didn't. It started to dawn on me that my brother is distinctively different from everybody else, and I often wondered why that was and what it meant. As I started to learn more about God, life and death, heaven and hell, I often wondered what that meant for somebody like David.

I used to innocently ask my mum, "Where would David go when he dies?" And her response was "heaven." Usually, I would accept this answer the same way I accepted everything at that point, but as I got older, this led to more questions.

Will he ever talk? If we pray, will he be able to talk? If he does start to speak, what does that mean? Can he leave his school and come to mine? When he comes, will he be in my class, or will he have to start from the beginning?

As I grew older, I found myself with more questions than answers; and as I tried to make peace and become accustomed to life with my brother, there was a consistent reminder that there are questions that don't have answers. David and I went to different schools, and because of this, naturally, we had our own social circles. Anytime somebody would find out that I had a twin, immediately they would say, "Why doesn't he come to school with you?" or "Do you guys play tricks on other people?" or "I wish I had a twin. It would be so fun!"

These remarks—as innocent as they were—always upset me because I knew I would have to explain that my brother has a condition I knew nothing about. At the same time, it reminded me my relationship with David could never be the way I would have wanted. As a young boy growing up, explaining autism was challenging for me to do. I mean, did anyone really understand? For every instance I spent trying to explain what it meant to other people, there might be 100 more instances of me trying to explain it to myself. I tried to make sense of it as much as I could, even with the limited knowledge I had at the time. I would often hear people refer to David as disabled, special needs, retarded; I didn't even really know what any of these things meant at the time. I always associated disability with a physical impairment, and I would try to answer these questions in my head.

> *Is he disabled? Well, no, because he can do everything that I can do except talk. Okay, so being autistic means that you can't talk.*

This was how I explained it to myself and others until David and I left year six and went to our respective secondary schools. While I was attending a mainstream school, David went to a school that had a special unit; he was one of six autistic kids. I remember going to visit his school for a gymnastics event, and I had a chance to meet some of the kids in his unit; to my surprise, they could all talk!

This caused me even more confusion.

If being autistic means that you can't talk, and everybody here that's autistic can talk, then what does it actually mean to be autistic? Why is my brother different? What's wrong with him? Why can't he talk? Maybe they've got it wrong, and it is something else.

This is how I thought for years. It was such a strange and unique situation, and I soon realised nobody around me could give me any answers. I remember asking my mum on multiple occasions what it means to be autistic, but I cannot remember one response I received back; it seemed so much bigger than what my brain could comprehend; there wasn't any reference for me to point to. I remember conversations with my mum, and she would explain to me that there were different opinions about this, none of which seemed to add up. One of these opinions was that autism was genetic, but this didn't make sense because wouldn't the fact that we are identical twins mean that we would both have it? Another opinion was it could be due to a traumatic birth. Again, this also didn't make sense because David was born naturally, and I was born via caesarean section. So, by that logic, wouldn't that mean that, if anyone should have it, it should be me and not David?

Nothing made sense, and it became very apparent to me at a young age that when it came to my brother, nobody had any idea of what they were talking about. I mean, it's not like it mattered to anybody else anyway. David wasn't their problem; he was ours. He was mine. He was my brother; it was up to me to figure out why he is the way he is, explain to other people how to treat him, how to know what upsets him, and as I learned, I could only hope that others would be sensitive and understanding to that.

David used to run away—a lot! I mean, as a child, I always took it for granted David would be found, partly because he always was found eventually, and because I was very unaware of the danger he was putting himself in. I can only imagine the stress it put my mum through! Everything at a young age seemed exciting; to me, it seemed as if David was living like a movie star! I mean, every time he ran away, there was a fuss made from the school, my uncles would always come around, police were involved, one time there was even a helicopter! I always wanted to attend the search parties, but most of the time, I had to stay at home with an adult and patiently wait until he came back. I was never worried about him because he always came back. For me, it was never a question of if he would be found, or even when, I was always more interested in the "where"—would David be in Asda, on a bus, or would he be hiding somewhere? I remember on one occasion when we visited a friend of my mother's. She had four kids, all of whom were older than us. At some point, David managed to go missing, and everybody split up to look for him; this was the rare occasion that I was allowed to be part of the search party. I felt like a detective—it was like a big game that David was playing with everyone, and I seemed to be the only one who enjoyed it as much as he did.

In 2011, I remember seeing a post on Facebook about an autistic boy who had gone missing in East London, and his sister was asking if anybody had seen him in the past two days. The picture was of a handsome, young black boy, and I saw my brother in that picture. I was saddened to read that he was found dead a few days later. I immediately thought back to the days that David used to go missing, and I put myself in my mother's shoes. The fears and worries I later grew up to have of David being alone in this cold world were based on situations I envisaged happening if he was ever alone. I still think about that young man from time to time, and as my heart breaks for that family, I have realised that my mum was dealing with that fear of David meeting that same reality every time he went missing.

Fears and Worries

When I look back to the incident when the pastor wanted to strap my four-year-old brother down to a chair, I can think of countless other incidents that bring me to the same thoughts I had growing up and perhaps will always carry with me: The worries and fears of how the rest of the world will perceive and treat my brother.

David sometimes lacks awareness of others around him, and as we were growing up, this was something I found both difficult to manage and emotionally draining. One time we were walking down the road, David accidentally brushed past a lady walking the other way. I instinctively pulled David to the side quite aggressively and stopped to apologise to the lady. I was used to apologising to strangers for David accidentally bumping into them or making a noise that visibly made them uncomfortable, even when he was minding his business and not actually doing anything to anyone. Sometimes, people were understanding. A lot of times, we just received a dirty look without a response. On this occasion, by the time I had turned around, the lady looked back at us and said, "Make sure you look where you're going, you f****** black monkeys!"

I didn't even acknowledge the racial slur; the weight of what she had said didn't hit me at that point due to the shock, and so I apologised once again and tried to explain David didn't mean to do it. But before I could, she walked away and left us standing where we were. I then grabbed David by the arm and harshly told him off for not looking where he was going. I didn't think of how he may have felt. It never even occurred to me whether he even understood what just happened. All

I could think about was the malice in that woman's eyes and the disdain in her voice. This wasn't another child saying some mean things about him. This was a grown woman who had looked at us and made a snap judgement on us based on a split second. And it made me feel ashamed of my brother. I was ashamed because no matter what he did, he was always causing so much trouble. The truth is there was nothing to be ashamed of, but I didn't know that. It also upset me for a different reason because at that point, I understood that if an adult could make that assessment when we are kids, what does that mean for the rest of our lives? If a grown woman perceived David as an angry black child, how would the world view him? What would happen one day if I wasn't there? How could he possibly defend himself if he ever got himself into trouble?

If you ever get a chance to meet David, you will see that he has such a warm personality and has such a happy outlook. Whilst this is something I love about my brother; this is also something that adds to my worries. I am no longer ashamed of my brother, but the concerns remain the same. Regardless of whether David is viewed as such an inconvenience that even at four years old, the only solution is to have him strapped down to a chair, or whether he is viewed as an angry black male who deserves to be racially attacked, David has no malice in his heart. Yet, the world will never fully accept him, or even care to try.

I remember overhearing a conversation with my mum, I was about eleven or twelve, and a member of our church told her the reason David is the way he is, is due to a sin my mum had committed; it was her punishment from God. I remember being angry but seeing how much it affected my mother was such an eye-opener to some of the abuse she may have experienced and the trauma she may be carrying herself. I managed to let it go, partly because at the time I didn't know the person who said it, and partly because I knew many of the people I looked up to in church vehemently disagreed with this statement—at that age, I felt that we had a lot of support and encouragement. But I have always kept that in the back of my mind. Upon reflection, the main thing that I take away from that statement was that, in the estimation of that person, my brother is nothing more than a consequence or an extension of my mother's wrongdoing. David wasn't given the dignity of being acknowledged as a human being with his own feelings. He can be perceived as many different things by many different people who make uninformed, snap judgements about him but have no idea of what he's really like.

Another fear of mine has always been to do with David's behaviour, and I feel I will always carry this trauma with me. Any time David was upset when he was young, he would scream at the top of his voice and start slapping himself in the face. We would often call these instances "episodes." These could happen at any point and at any place. Dealing with it at home was difficult enough because there didn't seem to be anything we could do to get David to calm down. Even when he did calm down, if he was still upset, there was the chance he would start again. Dealing with this in public was even worse. It didn't matter if we were visiting family, out shopping, traveling on public transport, or even on holiday in a foreign country; once David started screaming, there was nothing anybody could do, and it always generated stares from everybody who was around. The episodes were such a humiliating experience for me, and it was the thing I was most scared of happening. As my mum would try to calm him down, and I could see everybody stopping what they were doing and begin to stare at us in shock, horror, and disgust, I would often think, *How can I show my face in this shop again?* or *Please, can we just stay at home instead of going out?* My main concern was David would cause another scene, but another reason was going back to these places and seeing people who may have been there. As much as there was a possibility of my mum being seen and recognised, all that was going through my mind was, *I'm his twin! We look exactly alike! I will definitely get recognised*!

I always thought about what I was going through, and I never considered why David was even upset in the first place. As previously mentioned, David was always happy about everything, and so for David to be so upset, clearly there must have been something deeper. I have always wondered what goes on in David's mind, and if you ever see us together, you might sometimes find me randomly staring at him and wondering. I look back on all these instances. To comfort myself and give myself peace of mind, I choose to believe David had no idea of the abuse and treatment directed our way because of him. But then I fear that if he does have an idea, what that does to him mentally? And did that ever affect him when we were younger?

I felt this a lot growing up in church. During our younger days, any time David would have an "episode," people would look first, then go about their business. At that time, the church was used to David and were always willing to help in any way that they could. They never made a big deal about it, and it was something I look back and appreciate. As we got older and we started to grow, David became louder and stronger, and these episodes became a lot harder to manage. The episodes also started to become less frequent, which sounds like a good thing, but all it did was build up fear and anticipation in me as to when the next one would be. As the church started to grow and more and more people attended, people who saw David and I grow up started to leave. I realised not as many people in the church were familiar with David and had not witnessed an episode. I felt this shift when we were about thirteen, and one of David's episodes happened in the middle of our service. The whole room went quiet, and I saw the shock on people's faces; it felt different from when we were younger, and I started to realise that even in church, the one place I felt was safe, David wasn't fully understood. By that time, I had learned to take that as rejection or failure of acceptance. This carried on over the years, and birthdays and events we would normally get invited to, we were no longer allowed invitations due to David not being welcomed. Even though the reason wasn't always communicated to me, I always understood what it was.

What tormented me about the episodes was very often I could see it coming, but there was nothing I could do to stop it; I could only hope to try and get David to leave the room before it started. Many times, trying to get him to leave would make it worse, as David would loudly refuse, drawing even more attention. Even so, any time I saw a potential indicator that David might erupt, I would immediately start looking for an escape. If an escape wasn't possible, I would get a lump in my throat, butterflies in my stomach, sweaty palms, and rapid heart palpitations as I knew the inevitable was coming, and I couldn't stop it. To this day, even though David is a lot calmer, I still get all the same feelings when we're out in a public place or in a confined space with any amount of people. For example, in 2019, David and I were in church, and as I observed him, I noticed David suddenly go quiet and make a motion with his hand as if he was about to hit himself. This was one of the indicators that I used to look for. I immediately scanned around the building to see where the closest escape was, and then I looked around the church. I realised that David's last episode in church was about ten years prior and there were hundreds of people in the room who had never witnessed it before—this would've been a complete shock to those who knew us but knew nothing about that part of our lives. Even people who'd been around when we were growing up and witnessed it, it'd been so long they may not have any clue what to do. I started to think, *We're now fully grown adults, David is bigger and stronger than ever before. If we couldn't stop him as a child, we have no chance of stopping him as a grown man.* All these thoughts were racing through my head as I found myself unable to focus on anything else around me. I couldn't concentrate on the sermon; I couldn't sit down in peace and allow my mind to wander anywhere else. All I could think about was the next available opportunity to escape the room and take David home without any interruptions. I didn't want any chance for somebody to look at my brother differently, as if he was less than human, or look at me differently and feel any form of judgment or rejection.

As the dynamic in church shifted from a safe place to a place where I felt very vulnerable to judgment, the thought started to sit with me, that no matter where we were, David may never be accepted. I started to personalise the rejection—because he's my brother, my twin brother, if they reject him, they've rejected me.

My fear has often overwhelmed me, and made me see the worst in society, which I often feel can hinder opportunities for David to enjoy himself or for people to prove me wrong. Due to getting used to rejection, anytime I was invited somewhere, if I was with David, I would often refuse to go. I thought I was protecting David. In reality, I was probably protecting myself. Oftentimes, when we were out on the bus, and David was making a bit of noise, drawing too much attention, I would take him off the bus at the next available stop and walk the rest of the distance to our location, no matter how far it was. I'm naturally a shy person, so any time David drew any attention towards us, the embarrassment seemed unbearable. The thought of me going out is not something I naturally was inclined to do, so if I had to take David out to go somewhere, it was almost out of the question. I look back now and realise there were a lot of times when David was and has been accepted, and even at times when I would scold him for making a bit of noise, it would be people around me telling me to leave him alone and let him enjoy himself. As a natural mechanism, my instinct is not to silence my brother. Still, my experiences have told me that I need him to understand that when we're out in public, we have to act a certain way to not cause any trouble for ourselves. This is a lesson I've had to unlearn over the years, as I've realised I have internalised my own fears of rejection, and in turn may have denied my brother opportunities to go out and enjoy himself in places he may not have the luxury of doing without me.

Growing up, I didn't speak about issues I had. Although my experience in many ways doesn't differ from any other young black male living in South London, having David as a brother made my experiences even more unique. I had a particular fear I didn't feel I could share with anybody else. As a teenager, it was difficult to avoid the gang culture, violence, and acts of crime in the neighbourhood. Out of fear of worrying my mother, I would often keep things to myself. I remember countless times being approached—often with a weapon—for my phone, or money, or something I had. Many times, I would either run as an escape, or in a few instances, if I thought I had a chance or I didn't perceive there to be a weapon involved, I would take my chances and fight. On one occasion, in 2006, I was on the bus on my way home, when a boy I knew from primary school approached me—he was the year above me and was with another boy who I had never seen before. This boy was known in the area, but we had not spoken for years. He instantly recognised me and attempted to rob me for my phone and the money I had in my pocket. As we went back and forth, he threatened to beat me up and then said these words:

"I know where you live. I know what school your brother goes to!"

At that moment, I felt a chill through my body—this wasn't my first experience with somebody threatening violence towards me, but this was the first time it had now involved David. I reluctantly gave in, and they took the money that I had on me before allowing me to get off the bus. As I walked off, kissing my teeth, the boy said to me,

"Iggy, don't get rude. You know, coz I can find your brother, and kill him!"

I knew that he didn't mean it, and I was never truly scared or worried he would do anything to David, but it struck fear into my heart, not just about seeing him again—which I did—but more about those who didn't know that I was a twin. While David and I went to different schools, they weren't not far apart from each other. It was possible that if I had a problem with somebody, they could see David and think that he was me, especially if they didn't know he was a twin. This fear used to eat me up, and it affected me in every scenario; I didn't actively have to cause trouble with somebody; just being approached by random boys coming home from school and running away was enough for them to keep looking out for me. What if they saw David? How would he protect himself? To this day, the thought of David in pain breaks my heart—how could I live with myself if David was physically hurt and beaten up by somebody because of me? Who could I even tell about this?

Our Relationship

David and I were very close growing up, and even though we're both the same age (David is 17 minutes older than I am), I naturally took on the role of being the big brother, looking after him whilst my mum went to work, taking care of him where necessary, etc. I'm so grateful I had a sibling I grew up with, but I often felt as if I was alone. I wished to have a brother who was "normal" to share things with, get advice from, and even to help protect me at times when I had to defend myself in fights. I had a physical brother at home, but I also felt like an only child. I always loved him, but at times I resented him deeply. I would often think to myself, *For the rest of my life, this will be a burden I will have to bear.* At times, it felt like I had a brother, but more often, David just felt like a dependent I had to look after, and a responsibility I couldn't shake, which affected how I viewed him at times. I even remember wishing he was never born so I could live my life as my own individual without worrying about taking care of him. I felt like I had none of the benefits of having a brother but all the responsibility.

As brothers do, we used to annoy each other a lot, to the point where I would be ready to fight physically. Although David was slightly stronger than me growing up, he very rarely hit back. This frustrated me because I didn't want to bully or hurt my brother when I knew he didn't want to hurt me, but I didn't know how else to release my emotions. Now, I realise something that may have been obvious to others but didn't occur to me growing up: David has always looked up to me.

Our situation is unique because we're identical twins, but completely different. You could almost compare what David may have been like by looking at me. David has never wanted to be limited in what he does. He has always tried to follow me around; he used to copy my every move. If I ate two mouthfuls of food, he would do the same. He always tried to do anything I would do. This was normal to me, as he had always done this, but upon reflection, I realised I was probably the example David looked to. Everything about us appears to be the same, so there shouldn't be any reason why he couldn't do what I did. David has never allowed any kind of limitations to hold him back, whether it's taking the keys from my hand to open the door or making sure that he's the person to press the bell when we are getting off the bus. He has always wanted to do any little thing he could to display his ability to do the same things as me.

Growing up, David was taught Makaton in school as a means of communication. We used this when we were younger, and because of other family members, I was familiar with using sign language as a form of communication. David hated using it. Even though he couldn't form cohesive phrases, he would always try to speak to communicate and then use sign language as a last resort if we couldn't understand him. It used to frustrate me until I realised he wanted to talk because he could see me talk.

When I think about how much my brother looks up to me, it humbles me because I look at him and often envy him. Our experiences as children, even when David was the target and I was only peripherally involved, caused me to carry a lot of pain, bitterness, and resentment .When I look at David, he has always had such a positive outlook on life. It's so inspiring, and I often look at him in amazement and wonder what kind of example I may have set for him to follow.

As much as David has been dependent on me, I know that he would do anything he possibly could for me, which used to be a comfort for me. Growing up, David and I used to sleep in the same bed, and as a child, I was afraid of the dark. The worst-case scenario would be for me to get to bed and for David to already be asleep, as the light switch was so far across the room. I would often leave the light on, but if I was awake and my mum would come and switch the light off, I would hold on to my brother; I felt comforted knowing he was right beside me in the bed.

As much as I appreciated his support, there were instances when this went wrong. One day, we were getting ready to go to church, and David and I were playing upstairs in our room. I accidentally threw a ball outside of our window, and it got stuck in the fence separating our garden from our next-door neighbour's. I couldn't reach the ball from the window, so I decided to leave it and left the room. I subsequently came back in, and I saw David outside, hanging from the windowsill in our room, trying to get back up! I tried my hardest to pull David back up into our room, but I was not strong enough. We both tried everything we could, and I was so afraid of what would happen if David fell. I tried and tried to pull him through. Eventually, I lost my grip, and David fell. As my mum was washing the dishes in the kitchen, she saw David fall and injure his leg.

Similarly to the time when David got ran over, I was caught up in the excitement of the situation. It was such an interesting story to tell all my friends later that day! But a few days later, when we were in our room and David went to open the window, I went immediately to stop him from trying to get out. David was pointing at the ball! I had completely forgotten about the ball and realised that was the reason David was out there in the first place. Without me asking, David had tried to do something for his brother and put himself at risk over it.

Some part of me truly believes David could sense when I was unhappy and felt he was the reason for it, so he has always tried to do what he could to make me happy. I struggle to think about that because it wasn't something he should have ever felt, and it upsets me to think I may have ever made him feel responsible for something that he has never had control over.

David required a lot of attention growing up, which I understood, but it naturally meant less for me. There were key workers who would take him out to eat, to the cinema, and other places. Sometimes, I was allowed to go, but more often, I had to stay at home. David even travelled to America without me! I never blamed David for this though; I knew it wasn't his choice to leave me behind. Because I became aware David would do what he could for me—and the advantage he had—I would often make him ask my mum for something I thought she would refuse (e.g., a packet of crisps, biscuits, McDonald's, and anything else I thought she would consider if it came from David). I never saw it as taking advantage of him.

I wish I could change many things about our childhood, but I appreciated knowing that even though our relationship wasn't what I wanted in some senses, I couldn't ask for a person to love me more than my brother did. This protectiveness, in turn, has made me even more protective of him than maybe I would have been before. Not only because I don't want him to feel rejection or abuse from others, but I don't ever want to see somebody take advantage of his good nature. To this day, I get so defensive of David, it upsets me when somebody upsets him. Whether it's a stranger, somebody who has worked with him in the past, or a family member, if I feel as if they're talking down to David in a demeaning or patronising way, I always take offense to it and make my feelings known. The irony of it is whilst most people try hard to communicate thoughtfully with David, I don't think anyone else can understand him the way that I can. David has taught me that his condition shouldn't define him or limit what he can do or understand. So, in the past, when David would push back on using Makaton, to communicate with me like I would speak to our mother, I now find myself pushing back on someone trying to "dumb down" speech. I let them know he understands more than they think, and to treat David with the same respect they would treat me.

Impact on My Friendships

As a child, I had a very short temper. My peers knew how to wind me up, whether it was calling me names, trying to pick a fight with me, or at worst, saying something about David. I remember summertime 2001, and my mum sent David and I to a local play scheme. I didn't want to go because I knew I couldn't enjoy myself or make friends because I would have to spend all my time watching out for David and making sure that he didn't cause or get into any trouble. To my surprise, we enjoyed ourselves for the first couple of days, and I didn't run into any trouble. On the third day, a kid introduced himself to me. It seemed as though I was making a new friend, and so I was happy to talk to him, until he looked at David and then said to me, "Yeah, that's your brother, innit? He's like an idiot or something?"

As you would expect, I took offense to this and responded back by calling him an idiot, which led to a small dispute that had to be stopped by the adults in charge. I thought after this incident, if I steered clear of that boy, I would be fine. I didn't know that boy was very popular in that playgroup, so many of the children wouldn't speak to me after that incident. David and I spent the next week and a half isolated from everybody else and just playing with each other. Whilst I didn't particularly want to be around those kids, especially because that boy was amongst them, I felt very left out and resigned to the fact that as long as David was my brother, I wouldn't be able to make friends the way I wanted to.

I soon realised David wasn't the reason I struggled to make friends, but rather David exposed who my real friends were. In secondary school, David used to get picked up by a green bus provided by the Wandsworth Council. These buses were well known for transporting people with special needs; if you grew up in the Wandsworth borough, you would instantly recognise this bus. One time, I came into school and a few of my friends asked me if my brother took the bus. As I responded, I noticed a few of the boys in the background were laughing at me. When I asked why, they looked at me and then sarcastically said, "Nah, it's nothing. Yeah, your brother's a G!" and then carried on laughing.

At that point, I instantly realised they weren't asking out of genuine interest, but they were waiting to mock me about it, which hurt me. They could say anything about David, but they viewed my brother as something to laugh about and wanted to provoke a reaction out of me. These weren't just random kids I hadn't met before; these were boys I had gone to school with for three years and thought were my friends. I started to qualify my friendships and relationships based on how they responded to anybody with special needs. If they did anything insensitive, I would note to myself to keep them at arm's length.

Our Father

I've spoken about rejection from the world, whether it be abuse from a stranger or my complicated relationship with my peers, but this issue has a deeper root, starting with my father. My father didn't live with us, and like most boys, I idolised him. I remember any time he would call my mum, I'd rush to the phone and ask for a chance to speak with him. The few times he came to the house, I would be upset when my mum sent me to bed because all I wanted to do was spend time with him. I even remember staying up hours past my bedtime, waiting for him to come over like he said he would, and my mum sending me to bed when it became apparent he wasn't coming. I yearned for my father's love for years, and I idolised him.

My father was very inconsistent and wasn't somebody who would live up to his promises. So, I often found myself being let down by him often. However, on the few occasions he kept his word, I would be so happy to see him that I would instantly forget about all the times he'd promised and hadn't kept his word. I didn't realise that every time my dad came to see us, he was only really coming to see me. I overheard countless arguments with my mum and dad on the phone, and my mum would talk about how he needs to spend time with his boys and that anytime he bothers to show up, he only comes to see me, not David.

There was never an instance where David and I both went out with my dad unless my mother was around as well—which was rare. As this became more apparent, I started to lose the respect and adoration I once had for this man. As bad as it is, things started to make sense. If David's flesh and blood didn't accept him, what chance would he have with anyone else?

My dad had two sons younger than us. Growing up, we always wanted to see each other more; I didn't quite understand why we didn't spend more time together. As I got older, I started to wonder if that was intentional. I realised the damage this had on me growing up once I was a lot older, and I met my younger brothers by myself. On one occasion meeting M (one of my younger brothers), the first thing he asked was to see David, and how he was. His concern took me by surprise, and I realised I had assumed my dad's rejection of David had been passed on to my brothers, when in fact, they had always accepted him and had never felt the shame of having David as a brother in the ways I had felt it.

This was also one of many reasons my relationship with my dad broke down, and whilst he practically became a stranger to me, he had always been a stranger to David. After he passed away in 2019, I showed David a picture of him to see if he could tell me who he was. He looked at me very confused and said, "M?" Whilst there is a significant resemblance to our dad and our brother M, that highlighted to me that David had never known this man. Even though it was a relationship I missed, David never missed it.

When I was growing up, these experiences caused me to wrestle with two different sides of me; on one hand, I wanted to be accepted by the world, especially at a very young age, but I learned from my dad, my peers, and strangers that David was something I should be ashamed of, and I would never be fully accepted as long as he was attached to me. My longing for acceptance and my internalisation of this feeling caused me to blame David for holding me back in life and I often treated David as if he was in the wrong. I was so used to addressing his behaviour in public that it became normal for me to tell him off for making the slightest noise, even when he was minding his own business. I began to realise I was blaming my brother for something that wasn't his fault. I felt ashamed of myself for feeling that way, and I started to view the world differently: It was no longer about us trying to fit in, and I was no longer going to try and adapt to everyone else; that wasn't our responsibility. I didn't care to make people feel comfortable around me or to try to laugh off the jokes so I could have friends. It didn't matter if somebody made a joke or was dead serious. I started to treat everybody in the same way: if they had any problem with my brother or made any remarks about him, I didn't want them around David. They didn't deserve to be. I didn't even want them around me—and this had a significant impact on the friendships I made going forward.

Mistaken Identity

As kids, there was a lot of involvement from social services and other family support professionals in our lives. One of these organisations provided a siblings' group for children who had autistic siblings. This group was so beneficial for me, as I met other children close to my age who had similar experiences. Even so, when I compare David and I to my peers, I recognise the uniqueness of our situation. Although these kids also had siblings with autism, theirs were all significantly older or significantly younger. I wondered if they had to struggle with their sense of identity in the same way that I did. Outside the groups, I met other sets of identical twins; however, they didn't go to different schools in the same way David, and I did, and they didn't have to deal with one of their twins being autistic.

Because David went to a different primary and secondary schools, there are many people in David's life who know about me but have never met me, and a few who have no idea I exist! This goes both ways; not everybody I meet knows I'm a twin. It has nothing to do with being ashamed, but because it's something that has always been normal for me, it's not something I think to tell people about unless it comes up in a conversation. Either way, it has always made for interesting encounters when I go out.

David and I have often been stopped on separate occasions by people who may know one of us and have confused us with the other. On one occasion, someone stopped me when I was going to school. My school was about a mile away from David's, and whilst David travelled to school via a designated bus that picked him up from our home, the buses that went to our respective schools stopped at the same bus stop but then travelled through different routes. On this particular morning, time was against me; I was running later than I normally would. However, I knew if I caught the next bus, I stood a chance of getting into school on time. As I walked down the hill to get to the bus stop, I saw the bus approaching from afar and realised I would have to run as fast as I could to make it. I sprinted down the hill, ducking and dodging everything that was in my way, and as I finally approached the bus stop, I felt something hooking onto my bag and pulling back in the opposite direction. I turned around, confused, and to my bewilderment, it was a lady pulling me back, and she was yelling at me with urgency. As I tried to make sense of what was going on, I realised she was telling me to get on the bus behind, which happened to be the bus going to David's school. I didn't understand why she was telling me this, and I asked her repeatedly, "What are you doing?" Her response was, "You need to get on this bus to take you to school!"

By the time I figured out what had happened, my bus had long gone, and in a frustrated voice, I shouted, "I'm not David!"

The lady looked at me stunned, and as I proceeded to tell her who I was, she apologised and explained she thought David was lost. The lady was a former teacher at David's school and wanted to make sure he got on the right bus. The explanation didn't make me feel better for a few reasons: I thought she should have known I wasn't David the minute I opened my mouth to speak, and instead of arguing with me, she would have saved me a lot of time. I also thought she should've known David didn't take public transport to school. To make matters worse, I got to school late and had to explain the reason to my teacher. Although everybody in my class thought it was funny, my teacher didn't believe me and gave me a detention for lying.

I can't remember what that lady looked like, and I didn't catch her name. Still, if I could meet her again, I would thank her for what she did that day because although she was convinced I was somebody else and made me late for school, she showed that she cared about my brother by going out of her way to ensure he didn't get lost that day. Although it makes for a funny story today, it also epitomises the experience I have been accustomed to growing up.

There have been times when I was out, and I noticed people staring at me for no reason; growing up in South London in the mid/late 2000s, I learnt to be vigilant. Often, I would get paranoid if somebody was staring at me because oftentimes it meant trouble—many times they would approach me to ask about David. Once I clarified who I was, a pleasant exchange would always follow, and they would always ask how David was doing and then express their fondness for him. It's something I've always cherished, and I now look forward to those encounters, as it shows the negative meetings I had while I was with David may have been the exception and not the rule. It also showed me that David has a life completely separate from me, where he is happy, loved, and accepted. It felt strange being in the role of the "secret twin" and realising David had his own identity separate from me. It's made me hopeful that, even though I would always be there for him, David would be alright facing the world alone.

Closure

When we were fifteen, David changed schools. This was a very pivotal moment in our lives because David was moving to a boarding school outside of London. I didn't know how to feel about this at the time. David had gone to a respite home roughly once a month, so I was used to David not being at home on short occasions, whether for a weekend or a couple of days in the week. This move, however, meant David would be away from home most of the school term and limit our access to him, as he would be far away.

As much as we loved David, it was very challenging with him at home a lot of the time. As we grew and got bigger, it became a lot harder to handle. His move gave my mum and I a lot to consider; there would be many positives, such as my being able to focus more on my education and social life, but there were also a lot of questions. How would we know what was going on in the school? Would David be happy? David likes a consistent routine; how would he adapt to such a huge change of scenery? In my mind, the demographic in Kent seemed to be a lot less diverse than it was in London; David would already stick out by being black. If we were having problems in our area, what would happen to him over there? And who would be there to defend him?

I know for my mum especially, there were a lot of opinions from different people about what she should do, and whilst I believe most people had good intentions, it just made a tough decision even harder. It annoyed me other people thought they could judge my mum based on that decision when they had absolutely no idea what we were going through daily.

Before David moved to the school, we were able to visit and look around to see what we thought—my mind was slowly starting to ease. Not only were the facilities excellent, but the support staff was also very assuring, I got to meet a lot of the residents. It was the first time I had seen so many young autistic boys and girls that were actually like David. They made the same noises as David, they had the same facial expressions, and I started to feel as if this was a place that he could fit into, and it also helped to allay my doubts about his diagnosis. Because most of the kids I had met up to that point with autism could speak on some level. It not only had confused me about what autism was, it also gave me doubts that the doctors had misdiagnosed him and had just assigned him to the closest "label" that fit.

There was a young boy whom we knew from David's primary school. His older brothers also attended the same secondary school as me, so we knew the family well. When I saw that this boy had moved to this school, I felt a lot better about the move. The only question I had left was about David and if he was happy. One week after David moved in, Mum and I travelled to visit him. I had missed David a lot that week. The trip to Broadstairs via coach and train seemed to take all day—we couldn't get there fast enough! By the time we got to the school and saw David, he seemed so comfortable in his environment that he didn't even really seem to care too much that we were there to see him. This comforted me and assured me David felt at peace in this school, with kids who were like him, and with a school with the right resources to support him.

Being raised in a Christian home, church has always been a big part of our lives. I used to get asked about why God allowed David to be the way that he is, and it has never left my mind. There were times when the church would pray for healing, and they would pray for David. I always used to believe that after each prayer, there was a chance he would be healed, and whatever was wrong with him would just be "fixed." As time went on, and I realised it was looking less and less likely that he could ever be healed, I started losing faith in prayer and asking God for anything altogether. I remember being upset when they asked David to go to the front, as I felt like it was demeaning to him, drew attention to the fact that there was something wrong with him, and on top of it all, I thought it was a waste of time. As I questioned my faith, I remembered the words people said to my mum about

David being a consequence of her sin. I started to wonder if my disbelief was the reason behind David not being healed.

On one of our visits to see David at his new school, one of the workers approached us and asked us about church. He mentioned David had made it abundantly clear that church was important to him and was a big part of his life, and they had started taking David to a local church on Sundays. He also said he wasn't alone and that some of the other residents were going with him.

At that moment, a new thought occurred to me: What if David had a special calling in his life? Whilst I am naturally shy and am more of an introvert, David is very social and loves being around people; people have always been drawn to him because of this. What if David would draw people to God who only he would have access to and others couldn't reach. I don't know what God has planned for David, but I do know his life has a purpose, and whether I understand it or not, I could make peace with it.

When I compare today to when we were younger, there seems to be more of an awareness of autism; however, the spectrum is so wide, it's impossible to make a profile to fit all. I don't consider myself an expert in this field; I just know my brother and my experiences. I look at David today and see someone who has his own identity. Whilst he may never be fully understood by all, I will always worry about him being accepted. He has taught me a lot, and even though there were times when I wished things were different growing up, I wouldn't change him for the world.

Helpful Hints

Supporting Your Autistic Child's Siblings

Sibling relationships can be complicated at the best of times, and autism throws another layer of complexity into the mix. Just as in "normal" sibling relationships, there are positive and negative elements that come into play when you have autistic siblings.

Things to consider to ensure your neurotypical children don't feel left out and ignored:

- Family time—Activities the entire family can enjoy together to foster a closer relationship between siblings, for example: local parks, adventure playground, swimming.

- Sibling groups—These are especially good for older siblings. This is a space for them to express their feelings to people who "get it," without guilt or judgment. Contact your local or national autistic association to find details of these groups.

- Explain Autistic Spectrum Disorder (ASD) in age-appropriate language. Use simple descriptions and try to answer their questions honestly.

- Make time for one-on-one activities with your neurotypical child. If you can get respite care or someone you trust to look after your autistic child for a whole day or weekend, you will be able to spend longer periods of time with your other children.

- Manage negative feelings. Talk to your children and let them understand that it's natural to feel the way they do, and their feelings are legitimate. Reassure them and encourage them to express how they feel, but emphasize that feelings and actions are different things and negative behaviour is not acceptable.

- Encourage wider support networks. As parents, we know how important this is for us, and it's just as important for our children. Help them to foster relationships with other friends and relatives, professional relationships, youth clubs/centres, churches/faith groups, special interest groups where they can be themselves and express their thoughts and feelings without fear of judgment. It can help them reduce feelings of isolation and loneliness.

- Inform their teacher of the family dynamics. Often siblings of special needs children misbehave in school in order to get attention, or are withdrawn and do not engage in the classroom. If the school is aware of the family circumstances, they can offer support and help the child come to terms with their feelings. Many schools have counselling services, and can also signpost families to services that can help them.

- Establish family rules. Having an autistic child can be difficult in a family, and rules and structure are important for everyone. Setting boundaries makes children feel safe, no matter how much they test them. Rules help children feel capable and foster good behaviour. The key is to keep rules positive (have dos as opposed to don'ts), consistent, age appropriate, and with consequences.

CHAPTER 11

When Your World Turns Upside Down

Dealing with the Unexpected & Planning for the Future

In 2020, I'd been following the news like everyone else, slightly concerned, but not overly worried, about the information coming out of Wuhan, the latest "flu virus"—coronavirus. Little did I know that this would have a huge impact on my life, nation, and the whole world. For me, the realisation that this was much bigger than SARS, swine flu, or avian flu didn't hit until the end of January when a cruise ship was placed on lockdown in the Italian port city, Civitavecchia. Passengers were quarantined on-board because two Chinese nationals were feared to be carrying the virus. Over the next two months, the scenario played out on different cruise ships around the world: the MS *Braemar* off the coast of Cuba, the *Silver Shadow* near Brazil, the *Silver Explorer* in Chile, the *Golden Princess* just off New Zealand, the *Norwegian Jewel* in the Pacific Ocean, the *Pacific Princess* near Australia, and many more. Nations around the world started organising flights to repatriate their citizens from Wuhan after the lockdown in Wuhan had been lifted. The reality of the situation started to hit home.

People still didn't understand how much the whole world—and our individual worlds—would change. I half-joked to a friend about how all the disaster movies we'd watched were becoming a reality. I have a confession to make I succumbed to pressure and watched Contagion. The similarities to the current situation were incredible, and in my heart, I started preparing for the worst-case scenario as played out in the film.

That year, my birthday fell on a Sunday. David, Jonathan, and Rianna treated me to a meal at a Caribbean restaurant called Cottons. The restaurant was quiet and peaceful; there was only one other party there. Little did I know that that would be my last meal out for what would feel like a lifetime. My niece's birthday was two days later, on the 17th, and I went over to celebrate with the family. That was my last family gathering before lockdown commenced in the UK on the 23rd of March 2020. I felt I was living in a waking dream—this couldn't possibly be happening. The introvert in me thought, *"This will be easy, not a problem. I've got this"*. But watching the news every day made me feel anxious. And social media was the worst. I kept on seeing videos of people coming to blows over the last packet of toilet rolls. I thought,' *Really? Toilet rolls? What on earth is the world coming to?"*

But then the panic buying started. Supermarkets were running out of basic staples, such as toilet roll (yes, I know!), pasta, rice, tinned tomatoes, and antibacterial gel/hand sanitizers. Fortunately, old habits die hard, and I tend to bulk purchase non-perishable food and household items—having had two teenagers at home, you have to bulk buy, or you run out of supplies pretty quickly. I could afford to wait until the mad rush died down to top up my supplies.

Unfortunately, hay fever season starts around February/March; as soon as I saw the trees begin to blossom, I realised it would become an issue. People were already paranoid about the coronavirus, and any little cough would send people moving out of your way and scurrying out of your sight. I developed a dry cough in the back of my throat the same week they announced lockdown, and that meant I had to self-isolate for fourteen days. David couldn't come home.

After the announcement by Prime Minister Boris Johnson, I called David's home to discuss what to do about David's regular weekend trips home. The lockdown rules stated that people from one household unit weren't allowed to visit or contact another household. However, there was an exception for children of divorced parents who had joint custody. They were allowed to travel between the two-family household units only. We applied that exception to David as I felt strongly that at least one thing had to stay constant in his life to maintain his sanity. We also agreed to various stipulations; if David or I contracted any symptoms of COVID-19 while he was with me, he wouldn't return to the home until after fourteen days of self-isolation. Conversely, if he showed any symptoms at the home, he wouldn't come home to me until after self-isolating.

So, I didn't see David for two weeks, and he struggled. He couldn't understand why his entire world suddenly came to a halt. He couldn't go swimming, bowling, for walks, nothing! He was stuck indoors all day, every day. And he couldn't go home because his mum was ill. The staff created a Social Story to explain in simple terms about Coronavirus and how everywhere was closed because people were staying home to stay well. Unfortunately, this just made David more anxious. He followed staff everywhere and couldn't sleep. He was more on edge than usual and started having meltdowns more frequently. The self-injurious behaviours that would previously occur from time to time were happening several times a day.

Anything, everything, and nothing would set him off. The poor boy was completely overwhelmed and couldn't cope.

When he finally came home after two weeks of us not seeing each other (I'd spoken to him on the phone), my heart sank when I saw how much weight he had lost. David has an extremely healthy appetite, and growing up, was always referred to as the bigger—or fatter—twin. But now his clothes were just hanging over his gaunt frame. I felt terrible! As a mother, I thought I should've anticipated how difficult this would be for David and tried to find solutions earlier. I just couldn't get over how skinny he was! It became quickly apparent that his appetite wasn't the problem, but his anxiety levels were through the roof. He followed me everywhere—I always had a shadow trailing me. If I went to the kitchen, he was right behind me. He was stimming more frequently and intensely. He'd rock back and forth on the chair violently, and he developed a new verbal stim that almost sounded like he was ululating. The smallest thing would set him off, and he'd start hitting his face furiously—it was extremely upsetting to watch and to see his bloodied swollen lips in the aftermath.

My brother Axe, who was working in London when the lockdown was announced, worked from home with me. He hadn't seen much of this side of David, and certainly not at this level of intensity; he was extremely worried. I tried to explain that it was David's way of coping with everything going on and just telling him to stop wouldn't make much of a difference. Axe was also worried about my mental well-being as trying to help David deal with his issues consumed me. But this was just par for the course for me; just another aspect of being a mother.

The staff at his home had already informed me he hadn't been sleeping, but David's sleeping habits have always been an issue, so I hadn't given it too much thought. But his first night home, he was loud all night long! He's usually quiet, with bouts of vocalisations and/or jumping on his bed—but this behaviour was new, and if David wasn't sleeping, no one else was either. He'd lost the ability to mask.

Masking, or compensating, is something an autistic person does to try to pass as "normal." They do this to fit into society and do things we neurotypicals take for granted—maintaining relationships, holding down a job, not sticking out for being different, etc. Many autistic individuals feel they need to suppress or hide their true selves for people to see them as functional members of society. The strategies used vary from person to person: David mimics a lot; he looks to Jonathan in particular, but also me for cues on how to behave and other social cues. When we're eating, he will take mouthfuls of food simultaneously with us, drink his juice at the same time, and even get up at the same time. It's almost like we have our own little game called "synchronised eating"! But now, he was suffering from autistic fatigue or burnout. He couldn't find the resources within himself to fake being normal. Coping with the world was difficult at the best of times, but nothing made any sense to him because of the pandemic.

The current pandemic has given me time to observe, reflect, and understand my son a little better. Most people, if not everyone, are struggling to cope with the situation, and specifically with the lockdown. Mental health conditions like anxiety and depression are on the rise, relationships are suffering, domestic abuse is on the up, and watching the news for daily updates isn't helping. We see great acts of compassion juxtaposed with appallingly hard-hearted behaviour. People everywhere are finding it difficult to cope. This made me think about David and other neurodiverse people. They probably felt like this on a daily basis when things were "normal," and with the current crisis, these feelings of anxiety, not being in control, and fear of the unknown must have been massively amplified. I felt so helpless at my inability to help David through this.

    I was exhausted. I was in a fortunate position to have regular work coming in—many of my colleagues didn't have work. Roughly 90% of Sign Language interpreters are self-employed, so if we don't work, we can't pay the bills; getting government assistance is complex and long-winded. But working remotely was mentally draining. I couldn't understand why my body refused to co-operate with me by the end of the day—I found it physically difficult to move. I later found out that Zoom fatigue is a real thing, and it's exacerbated in Sign Language interpreters because of the extra concentration needed and the added demands for processing in and out of each language.

    On the days I didn't work, I'd get out of bed at midday—only because my bladder forced me to make a run for the ladies! I'd grab something to eat, then watch TV for the rest of the day. My routine was sleep, wake up, shower, work, eat, sleep, repeat. In the early days of lockdown, I had many evening Zoom calls: informal/formal CPD – professional development sessions -to get to grips with the new way of working, supervision sessions, weekly check-ins with my peer supervision groups, virtual choir practice, family and friends checking on my welfare—no wonder I was worn out!

I called the manager of David's home after he'd returned to discuss David's health and well-being. They had taken him to see the GP, who wanted to prescribe him a low dose of Lorazepam, an anti-depressant, to help him relax and sleep. I've always been anti-medication when it came to David; I've never wanted him to be drugged up just to make other people's lives easy. But this time was different; he was struggling and suffering. I agreed, and a couple of days later, they called me to tell me it was helping, and he was sleeping better. He was a lot more mellow and much more his usual cheeky self. The following weekend when he came home, I could see the difference; he was still following me everywhere, repeatedly asking when he could do things like go for a haircut, go to church, go on holiday, etc., but he was more cheerful, cheeky, and he actually slept.

Shortly before lockdown, I spoke to David's home manager about planning for the future. She had already started conversations with some of the older parents about what would happen to their adult child after they'd passed on and agreed to set up an appointment with specialist advisors.

However, coronavirus happened, so everything was put on hold; the key priority was looking after the autistic individual's health and well-being. At the peak of the pandemic, looking at the numbers of people contracting and dying from COVID-19 and being aware that I'm in a high-risk group (black, over 50, and slightly overweight), I realised that I couldn't keep putting it off. I knew Jonathan would always look out for his twin, but he has his own life, and I didn't want David to become an obligation or burden that he would resent. I started researching and found an excellent toolkit on the Sense website called "When I'm gone; decisions to make, steps to take."[15] I have started going through the steps, and even though I haven't completed my plan, I'm feeling much better. I've included David by asking him about his likes, dislikes, plans, and hopes. I'm also keeping Jonathan in the loop, as he will be responsible for David after I've gone. When things are a bit more settled, I will also take legal advice, and meet with the specialist advice service to make sure I haven't left anything out. But for now, I have peace of mind, knowing that I'm doing my best to make sure both my boys will be okay once I'm gone.

Wonderfully Complex

Did You Know?

Legally Caring for Adults with Special Needs

As our special children transition into adulthood and begin to get older, we start to think about their future and the decisions that need to be made on their behalf. In the United Kingdom, there are three things we need to know when we think about advocating on behalf of our loved ones. Once a child with special needs or disability becomes an adult, the authorities and professionals in their lives don't have to consider the wishes of the parents when it comes to making important decisions unless they have one of the following decision-making powers:

Power of Attorney:

A legal document where a person nominates a trusted friend or relative to look after their affairs if they lose the capacity to do it themselves. The person must have the capacity to make this decision for it to be granted.

Guardianship:

Legal authority granted by the courts to make decisions on behalf of another person who is unable to make decisions in their best interests, provide for their own welfare, and unwilling or unable to sign a durable power of attorney. The guardian has the power to manage property, finances, and personal welfare.

Deputyship Order:

When a person has lost the ability to look after their affairs but has not set up a Power of Attorney beforehand, their carers can apply to the Court of Protection, and a deputy will be appointed to look after the person's affairs. There are two types of deputies: one for property and financial issues, and one for personal welfare.

It's advisable to apply for a deputyship before your child is sixteen, as it's a laborious process, which becomes more complicated after adulthood.

Helpful Hints

Making Plans for the Future

Sometimes, the thought of trying to make plans for when you can no longer look after your loved ones can be overwhelming, and you don't know where to start. The Sense toolkit[12] outlines various areas that you need to consider when planning for their care after you're gone. Just knowing what you need to consider and where to go to get the help you need makes a big difference. This is a summary of the different areas covered in the toolkit:

1. *Where will they live?*
   - *Residential care*
   - *Supported living*
   - *Home care (independent living with help)*
   - *With family/friends*
2. *Who will pay for this?*
   - *Social Care*
   - *Direct Payments*
   - *National Health Service (NHS) – Personal Health Budget (PHB)*
   - *Savings*
3. *What finances will they have? Money from:*
   - *Wills*
   - *Trust*
   - *Benefits*
   - *Grants (e.g., Disabled facilities grant)*

4. Who will look after their interests?
   - *Professional (independent) advocates*
   - *Peer advocates*
   - *Circle of support*
   - *Power of attorney*
   - *Deputy*
   - *Care Act*
   - *Guardian*

5. How can I find support for myself now?
   - *Carer's assessment by local authority*
   - *Carer's allowance (depending on eligibility)*

Afterword

Thank you so much for staying the course as I've shared my journey of raising my boys to adulthood. Many things have changed since David's diagnosis—there's a greater awareness of Autistic Spectrum Disorder and an increase in diagnosis and statements. Unfortunately, some things haven't changed. It's increasingly difficult for parents to get the education provision they prefer for their children. Even if they manage to get a statement of educational needs, there's no guarantee the child will receive the support they need.

Awareness has increased, but attitudes have not improved. When David was younger, I didn't have the energy or capacity to look more than a year ahead and think of his future. Sometimes, I feel immense sadness about what he is "missing out on." My dreams for David are completely different from my dreams for Jonathan. But ultimately, I want my sons to be happy, fulfilled, and content. This means different things for both of them.

David wants to work; he wants to be a productive member of society. But because of how his autism presents, it's challenging; it's a work in process. He also wants to live independently—he has shown me buildings and apartments and told me "David's house." In the past, I've fobbed him off, but while writing this book, my thinking has started to shift. As a mother, I tell myself I will support my sons to help them fulfil their potential. Maybe I've been underestimating David for a long time. When people ask me about David's skills and abilities, I've said he can do more than the experts and professionals think, but maybe he is capable of more than I think as well. Perhaps I've been wrong and slipped into that trap of thinking I know my child better than he knows himself.

Before the strange events of 2020, David was trying to do what Jonathan had done years ago—grab the apron, run with it, and throw it away. I've learned I need to let him go, be independent of me, and be a man. Yes, he will make mistakes, but that's part of life, and he has a great support system around him, including his brother and myself. No, it won't be easy, but nothing worth having comes easy. Part of the responsibility being a parent is to equip your child, so they need you less and less. My children are not an extension of me, as much as I hate to admit it.

My vision is to help parents, siblings, and family members of children and young people with autism navigate some of the challenges I went through. Now that I'm on the other side, I can look back and see how I could have approached things differently. I'm not an expert (just an expert on my son), but I'm further along on my journey. My hope is to help parents avoid some of the pitfalls I came across. I am a trained Parent Advocate and support parents and carers in Child in Need and Child Protection Conferences. My deepest wish is no parent should feel alone - I want to support parents in the same way I would have liked to have been supported when I started this journey with my sons.

I have also written a children's book exploring an autistic child's sibling's experience called "Adventure at the Seaside." I'd love to hear your thoughts. Please contact me on: www.tayoigbintade.com for further updates on what I'm up to.

Bibliography

Abang, Theresa B. "Disablement, Disability and the Nigerian Society." *Disability, Handicap & Society* 3, no. 1 (1988): 71-77. https://doi.org/10.1080/02674648866780061.

"ATN/AIR-P Strategies To Improve Sleep In Children With Autism" Autism Speaks. Accessed December 1, 2020. https://www.autismspeaks.org/tool-kit/atnair-p-strategies-improve-sleep-children-autism.

Bakker, Peter. "Autonomous Languages Of Twins." *Acta geneticae medicae et gemellologiae: twin research* 36, no. 2 (1987): 233-238. https://doi.org/10.1017/s0001566000004463.

Barry, Kevin, Robert Francis Kennedy, and Boyd E Haley. *Vaccine Whistleblower: Exposing Autism Research Fraud at the CDC*. New York, NY: Skyhorse Publishing, 2017.

Burkett, Catina. "'Autistic While Black': How Autism Amplifies Stereotypes: Spectrum: Autism Research News." Spectrum, January 20, 2020. https://www.

spectrumnews.org/opinion/viewpoint/autistic-while-black-how-autism-amplifies-stereotypes/.

Clayton, Darla. "20 Things Every Parent Of Kids With Special Needs Should Hear." Accessed December 1, 2020. https://www.abilities.com/community/parents-20things.html.

Commission on Race and Ethnic Disparities. The report. Mar 2021. https://assets.publishing.service.gov.uk/government/uploads/system/uploads/attachment_data/file/974507/20210331_-_CRED_Report_-_FINAL_-_Web_Accessible.pdf.

"Communication." Accessed October 22, 2020. https://www.autism.org.uk/about/communication/communicating.aspx.

Davis Smith, Jamie. "Eight Things Siblings Of Children With Special Needs Struggle With." The Washington Post, April 21, 2019. https://www.washingtonpost.com/news/parenting/wp/2016/12/20/8-things-siblings-of-children-with-special-needs-struggle-with/.

Etieyibo, Edwin, and Odirin Omiegbe. "Religion, Culture, and Discrimination against Persons with Disabilities in Nigeria." *African Journal Of Disability* 5, no. 1 (2016). https://doi.org/10.4102/ajod.v5i1.192.

Ghose, Tia. "Parents Of Autistic Kids Have Higher Divorce Rate." Milwaukee Journal Sentinel, September 8, 2010. http://archive.jsonline.com/news/health/100266159.html.

Kosminsky, Pam. "The Double Discrimination Facing Black Children With Autism." Black Ballad, December 20, 2019. https://blackballad.co.uk/views-voices/double-discrimination-black-children-autism?listIds=594c1056f818c22c414c4995%2C597d7d9227ae01692833fe86.

Miles, M. "Some Influences of Religions on Attitudes Towards Disabilities and People with Disabilities."

Journal of Religion, Disability & Health 6, no. 2-3 (2002): 117-129. https://doi.org/10.1300/j095v06n02_12.

Silberman, Steve. "Science, Race, and the Invisibility of Black Autism." Undark Magazine, September 30, 2019. https://undark.org/2016/05/17/invisibility-black-autism/.

Stebbins, Leslie. "Autism Parents: How Do You Rate on Self-Care?" Autism Resources and Community (ARC). Accessed October 22, 2020. http://blog.stageslearning.com/blog/autism-parents-self-care.

"The Triad Of Impairments." Galway Autism Partnership, May 23, 2018. https://www.galwayautismpartnership.com/the-trid-of-impairments/

Endnotes

1. Wakefield AJ, Murch SH, Anthony A, Linnell J, Casson DM, Malik M, et al. Ileal-lymphoid-nodular hyperplasia, non-specific colitis, and pervasive developmental disorder in children. Lancet. 1998;351: 637–41. [PubMed] [Google Scholar]
2. https://www.autism.org.uk/advice-and-guidance/what-is-autism
3. Diagnostic and Statistical Manual of Mental Disorders : DSM-IV. Washington, DC :American Psychiatric Association, 1994.
4. Wing, L. Language, social, and cognitive impairments in autism and severe mental retardation. J Autism Dev Disord 11, 31–44 (1981). https://doi.org/10.1007/BF01531339
5. Whitehead, Andrew L. "Religion and Disability: Variation in Religious Service Attendance Rates for Children with Chronic Health Conditions." Journal for the Scientific Study of Religion 57(2): 377-95.

6   Erik W. Carter, Equipped for Inclusion: Western Theological Seminary's Graduate Certificate in Disability and Ministry, Journal of Disability & Religion, 10.1080/23312521.2021.1895022, (1-18), (2021)
7   YMCA. Young and Black: the young Black experience of institutional racism in the UK (2021) https://www.ymca.org.uk/wp-content/uploads/2020/10/ymca-young-and-black.pdf
8   Peretti, Frank. This Present Darkness: A Novel. United Kingdom: Howard Books, 2012.
9   Peretti, Frank. Piercing the Darkness: A Novel. United Kingdom: Howard Books, 2012.
10 https://iancommunity.org/whats-truth-about-autism-and-marriage
11 https://archive.jsonline.com/news/health/100266159.html
12 *https://www.sense.org.uk/umbraco/surface/download/download?filepath=/media/1972/campaign-when-im-gone-decisions-to-make-steps-to-take-a-guide-to-planning-long-term-care-and-support-for-disabled-adults-and-their-families.pdf*

Acknowledgements

There are so many people I'd like to thank for their support over the years, I hardly know where to start. My siblings Akin, Kunle and Tina, who have been there for me from day one – I don't know how I would have managed without you. I'm eternally grateful for your continued support. My entire family – the Igbintade, Beyioku, Adekanmbi, Oketoki and Ogundeji families – thank you for your emotional and moral support through the years. Even when you didn't understand what was happening with David, your unwavering, unconditional love and acceptance got us through the tough times.

I thank God for my tribe; my friends and spiritual family that God has blessed me through the years. There are too many for me to count, but I'll attempt to Stephen Adewole, Alex Adewole, Toks Aroture, Pastor Marty Carnegie, Sandra Simeon, Primrose Betera, Peter and Paulette Billings, Vivienne Adesanya, Errol and Teresa Lodge, Baba, Will and Folusho Olusanya, Timi Ogunyode, Vivienne Adesanya, Louisa Coulthurst, Tracey Duru, Timi Ogunyode, Sarah Otto,

Anthony Mateus, Edward and Sia Kanu, Pastor Simeon and Harriet Oshungbemi, Pastor Jamille Hurst, Pastor Collin, Pastor Jay Nembhard; thank you all for your emotional support, your practical assistance and your prayers and spiritual guidance. It really did make a difference

My church family: a special mention goes to Monalisa and Femi Sofolarin, Tendai Mizha, Koockie Kim, Angela and Patrick Pope, Joy Onyegbosi John Tan, and Lena Loh.

The Igniting Souls Tribe, especially the London chapter, with a special mention to Karin Brauner Hollman for walking me through the technical bits, and Andy Beck my accountability partner.

The PPP children's author group for your emotional and moral support when I started to get discouraged towards the end; a special thank you to Andrew L Ramirez for his motivational talks, and to Gemma Bond, Jo Blake, Patricia Maiorano and Caroline Milmine for your pep talks, and talking off the ledge when I felt like giving up.

My editors and Beta readers, who help me with the writing Jill Ellis, Bethany Peat and Chris Rolfe. Monalisa Sofolarin, Sarah Otto, Shaunett Harris, Vivienne Adesanya and Anthony Sheehy.

The igniting Souls London (author) group for inspiring, pushing, and encouraging me when I felt like giving up. A special thanks to Karin Brauner Hollman for helping me through some of the trickier processes, and Andy Beck, my accountability pest (only joking), for getting me through when it seemed like procrastination was winning the battle.

The PPP (children's author) group, who have supported and cheered me along the way. Thank you, Gemma Bond, Jo Blake and Caroline Milme, for checking with me when it seemed like I'd fallen off the face of the earth. A huge thanks to Andrew L Ramirez for helping me find the children's book that I didn't know was inside me.

To everyone who has supported me along the way - a huge thank you.

About the Author

Tayo Igbintade has navigated health, education, and social services for nearly 30 years while raising her autistic son and his neurotypical twin. She became a passionate advocate for autistic children and adults during this time. Tayo took this passion to the public arena by supporting a fellow parent, Ivan Corea, in his successful campaign to have 2002 declared Autism Awareness Year in the UK. She also participated in a steering group for the National Autistic Society in their efforts to better support their first BME (Black and Minority Ethnic) Steering group. She continues to work with parents to support their autistic children to thrive and reach their full potential.

Tayo is employed as a British Sign Language/English Interpreter in a range of settings. She is also a parent advocate who support parents of children with special educational needs. She is an author and speaks on autism related topics, especially about how autism intersects with faith, culture, and religion. Her children's book, *Adventure at the Seaside* was published in Spring 2021.

Tayo lives in South London near her twin sons, who share her love of holidays and all things to do with tourism. She loves reading, Star Trek (but not Star Wars), criminal procedurals and cake.

Jonathan Ogundeji is the identical twin brother of an autistic adult. He has a passion for working with vulnerable children and young people and works with young people in the areas of domestic abuse, gangs work and child criminal exploitation.

He is a co-founder of Bridge the Gap Studios; a social enterprise that works with young people in London who are facing challenging life situations.

Are you ready to join a community of like-minded parents, and become equipped to advocate for your child's needs?

Welcome to Audacious Advocates, where you will learn to

- Affirm your child and speak positive words into their life, so they can understand that they have been created for a purpose and can be secure in who they are,
- Appreciate your child and understand that they still have a potential to fulfil, that you can support them with
- Advocate for your child and learn how to speak up for your child and get the resources and support you need to help them fulfil their unique potential.

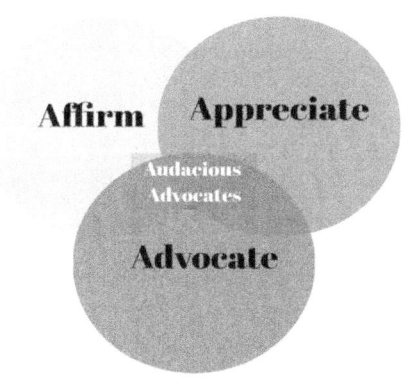

Join our private Facebook group, Audacious Advocates where you will join a community of like-minded parents, receive and offer peer support and access to resources to help you support your child.

Printed in Great Britain
by Amazon